D0426340

Dying Unafraid

Dying Unafraid

by

Fran Moreland Johns

SYNERGISTIC PRESS
San Francisco

Copyright © 1999 by Frances Moreland Johns

All rights reserved.

Printed in the United States of America.

Dying Unafraid's interior typographic design is by Marin Book-works, San Rafael, CA, which set the text in Adobe Caslon. It was printed by Thomson-Shore, Dexter, MI. The jacket design is by Debra Turner, Sausalito, CA, and features Richard Mayhew's oil on canvas painting, *Spiritual Transition* (1997), provided through the courtesy of ACA Gallery, New York City.

First edition
0 9 8 7 6 5 4 3 2 1

Library of Congress Cataloging-in-Publication Data

Johns, Fran Moreland, 1933-
   Dying unafraid / by Fran Moreland Johns
     p. cm.
   ISBN 0-912184-11-6
   1. Death.   2. Conduct of life.   3. Death—Case studies.
4. Conduct of life—Case studies.   I. Title.
BD444.J554 1999   98-40523
155.9'37—dc21   CIP

Synergistic Press
3965 Sacramento Street
San Francisco, CA 94118

In loving memory of

Helen and Earl Moreland

Laurette Fossett

and

Isabel Johns

who knew how to live boldly and die unafraid

Contents

Changing Your Mind   1

A Sense of Place   11

Making Peace   24

A Moment in Time   39

Listening to the Nightsong   47

Celebrations of Life   56

Self-Deliverance   65

Mystery and Meaning   75

Big Gifts from Small Sources   87

Beholding Beauty   97

Creative Impulses   105

The Spirit of Laughter   119

Who's in Control Here?   129

Private Choice, Public Dilemma   137

Models   154

Changing Your Mind

I used to pretend I would never really die.

That is not, after all, such an unusual stance. I always had company among other people eager to talk about anything else, eager to enter into the same pretense. I took pains not to think about dying very much, and was particularly careful not to watch it happen. If I did not talk about it, or see it, or spend time around anyone else doing it, pretending that dying would not happen to *me* was easy.

The business of dying is much more attractive when viewed through a filter of one's own assumed immortality. I was as good at that as the next person. It allowed me to have the average amount of morbid curiosity about terrible accidents and major catastrophies, while keeping a secure distance.

So I surprised even myself, somewhat, when I first signed up to be a hospice volunteer. It was in the early 1980s, when the American hospice movement was still young and many of us working in the movement were nervous about everything: about confidentiality, about getting involved with government, about trying to convince people that dying itself might not be the worst thing that comes to our lives.

Most of all, I was nervous about being around dying people. Years earlier I had spent a good bit of time doing volunteer work at a county-run home for the elderly and chronically ill. When people I knew there died I was sometimes nearby, but there was a space that separated us, a cushion of safety.

In the years between my experiences at the nursing home and my entry into hospice volunteer work I had had an average number of encounters with death—generally the deaths of family or friends—for someone in her early fifties, as I then was. But holding hands with dying strangers? Mopping foreheads? Hugging closely and listening to rasping, dying words and final, gutteral sounds?

Frankly, it was a scary idea. But I managed to stay in the classes and finish the training, and plunged almost immediately into my first case—a woman I will call Joan. She was a soft-spoken farmer's wife whose grown children had an unabashed affection for her, and who still retained the dark-haired beauty that had first attracted her husky, weather-worn husband.

Although she underwent treatments recommended for her cancer, Joan balked at institutional care. She saw herself not as waited-upon but as waitress. Until a short time before her death Joan would get up to greet me at the door, trailing IV tubes on portable hangers, offering coffee or tea.

The family moved Joan, eventually, into a sunlit living room, with the side of her hospital bed near the picture window. She spent her dying days there, in and out of a coma, usually with grandchildren climbing up on the bed, saying, "Can I show you something, Grandma? I made a picture in playschool today. Here, see?"

That kind of a dying will go a long way toward changing your mind about a process you had called The Grim Reaper. Other kinds of dying have changed my mind even more. "Jane Roe," arguing eloquently into a video camera for a change in the prohibition against physician-assisted dying in the state of Washington because she knew that she herself, a physician with cancer, would not live long enough to argue her case in court—she and others in that arena have changed my mind about physician-assisted dying. The law may remain, but it is still worth listening to those whose bodies are failing yet whose minds know that dying holds no fear. Their stories speak loudly to the living.

A number of young men I have known and loved while working with an AIDS support group have changed my mind about self-deliverance. Others have made me rethink the whole business about whether we need to be somber around the dying. Still others, in their dying, have encouraged me to consider the wisdom of making peace amid broken relationships today, just in case I might find myself dying tomorrow.

Many of those who have changed my mind are people I have never even met, people whose survivors have shared their stories with me when they heard about this book, or people who did such an uncommonly fearless job of dying that they wound up in other books. Some of them *wrote* books.

Still, changing one's mind, especially on a subject as near to the heart as one's own demise, is not an easy thing to do. So I am grateful to all of the above and many more for the fearlessness with which they demonstrated that dying may not, after all, be the worst thing that ever happens to us. Their stories, recounted here, have the power to change many minds, to open all of our eyes.

"You know, people think dying is some big bad thing," Vetris used to say. "I disagree." Then her huge brown eyes would sweep the room, twinkling almost imperceptibly as they passed my face, as if registering the suspicion that I might not catch on. And she would grin at no one in particular. "I know whose child I am," Vetris would say.

Vetris was one of the people who first showed me that death is something one can finally embrace, after pushing it away until pushing no longer works. She was a hospice patient of mine, whom I first met in what turned out to be the last six weeks of her life. In those weeks, though, I got a generous portion of Vetris' ebullient philosophy of living and dying.

When I initially encountered the unfeared death it was personified by people who, like Vetris, were all near or past retirement age, and who shared at least three or four major similarities. Each had a strong religious faith, each had accomplished at least a few life goals, felt his or her affairs to be acceptably in order and had no one (child, spouse, close friend or business associate) pleading with the dying person to hang on just a little longer.

Aha, I thought. If I were to collect a hundred stories of people who died unafraid, the threads of those stories would reveal strong corollaries of elements such as the above. I had in mind the creation of a blueprint, of sorts, a set of disciplines pointing straight toward "the good death."

Something strange and fascinating happened, as I slowly proved myself wrong. It was the discovery that there may be no such thing as "the good death", that death may always be, in part, an unwelcome stranger. But the search for ways to participate more fully in the living-and-dying process lies along a pathway that hundreds, perhaps millions, have walked with sure feet. And they have left markers.

For tiny, tough-as-nails Vetris, death was neither totally unwelcome nor strange. Vetris, when we first met, was bald from chemotherapy and unable to walk. She had suffered an incredible assortment of maladies that contributed to her body's being wasted and useless. We were immediate best friends, a state of grace that was easy to reach with her.

Vetris had huge brown eyes that seemed all-knowing, skin the color of dark mahogany and the texture of crushed velvet. Her skin looked as if it had been delicately stretched across her angular skull and her eyes then set carefully into their elliptical sockets like two gleaming copper and pearl jewels. The perfect order of her face, under its bald pate, was in sharp contrast to the disorder of virtually every other part of her body.

Vetris had been a pioneer leader among black school staff personnel in her community, in the early days of integrated schools in Florida. She had also been a significant leader/role model for family and friends, and was now a force to be reckoned with if any of them did something she deemed inappropriate. I remember a young niece visiting early one Sunday afternoon, seeking to bring cheer to her dying aunt and instead getting a lecture about skipping church. Almost into the very moment of her death she was going about the business of living as she had always enthusiastically, emphatically lived.

Just about the only thing that worried her, Vetris told me, was that some of her family and friends "were taking this too hard." That's when she would follow up with the no big bad thing commentary.

Other than worrying about those who worried over her, Vetris spent her last days—the days of her dying—concentrating on the immediate task at hand. Severely crippled in her legs and torso, paralyzed on one side and unable to use her right arm or hand, she was teaching herself to write with the left. A week or two before she died she mastered the art of writing a fairly legible version of her name, and was printing words that slanted around the page a lot but could certainly record her thoughts.

I would find Vetris propped up in a chair that had a writing desk attached, an old cigar box full of pencils and note paper on the desk beside her useless right elbow, observing the world and recording what she felt significant. "You see," she explained to me one day, "I want to make every day better than the day before."

When Vetris died, they told me she had a pencil in her left hand. I did not know if that were just something the nurses, who had grown to love her and her gumptious ways, made up, but I wanted to believe it a fact. Vetris had few possessions at the nursing home, but I put the cigar box on the gurney before the funeral home people came, and suggested maybe it should go into the casket. If Vetris wanted to print her way, left-handed, into the hereafter, I did not want to be caught impeding her progress. In those last weeks she had, furthermore, convinced me that death for her represented exactly that: progress.

For someone like Vetris, who was not "old" but had led a full and rewarding life, it is often easy to see death as progress, as more good than bad. It is also possible, perhaps, to be more easily accepting of death when one is a grandmother or a retiree or a Nobel Prize winner. But the fact is that many others, young people raging at the injustice of it all, adults in their prime with important goals yet to reach, still manage to face death unafraid. The mystery of how that happens may be much easier to untangle than the mystery of death itself.

Often it is the dying who come closest to unraveling that mystery for us, the living. One cannot listen to the conversations of young men with AIDS as they trade information about stockpiling potentially life-ending drugs, or the voices of those whose dying words are arguments for changing physician-assisted dying laws, without learning that death is not the ultimate fear. It's hard to read the parting one-liners of comedians (some professional, some not) as they played to their final audiences without learning something about using familiar skills to help smooth the passage into unfamiliar territory.

Laughter and pain, struggle and perseverance are familiar; death is the ultimate Unfamiliar. But like it or not, we are all dying. Death is a process, the experts say, that begins with our arrival on earth and moves right along until our departure. We can accelerate the process by smoking cigarettes, by eating or drinking unwisely or subjecting our bodies to an assortment of other physiological abuses; we can perhaps slow it down by taking vitamins or practicing tai chi. But we can't reverse the course. Sooner or later, this is what we all do: we die.

Maybe if we look it in the eye, as people like Vetris have shown us how to do, our own death won't be such a big bad thing.

I believe Lona Jones, a life-loving and courageous nurse with brain cancer who chose to seek help in dying from Dr. Jack Kevorkian because she knew the next seizure could take away her ability to make choices, also looked death in the eye and found it not the ultimate fear. I think the same might be said for Moliere, gasping through his own dying moments while delivering the lines about sickness and death, real and imagined, that he himself had written. And I think it could easily be said for two friends quoted by Georgia hospice worker Anne Harris: the Jewish lady who said her death was "just an ordinary part of my life; not something I want to do, but a part of my life" and the Zen Buddhist who said of the birth/death cycle, "Make peace; tie up loose ends; that makes 'good death' possible."

Undoubtedly, the irrepressible writer/activist/debunker of all things pompous Jessica Mitford saw something potentially grand, a new world to conquer, in going to her own rewards. She went without fanfare from the funeral industry she had done battle with and profoundly changed. Naturalist/writer Sigurd Olson typed a parting line, just moments before his death in the wilderness he loved, about "a new adventure coming up . . . " I think they each died unafraid.

We don't talk much about "good death," or whether there even is such a thing. We talk about loss, and working through grief. We see others' dying mostly through our own sadness, pain, guilt and sometimes anger; any of those are easier than the lens of our own mortality. Sometimes, though, they can distort a clear and simple message.

A few years ago a fairly prominent southern couple took a look at their earthly future and didn't like what they saw: one was well into a debilitating illness with death a nearby certainty and the other had just been diagnosed with a disease that would soon lead to loss of function.

So they tape-recorded messages to their family and friends, lit candles, put on a recording of their favorite symphony, shared glasses of their best wine and then died together, of gunshot. Their deaths made all the papers, and the story was in radio and TV reports across the state.

In every report I heard or read the incident was referred to as "the tragic deaths" or "the tragic murder-suicide" of Mr. and Mrs. X. I disagree; and I suspect they would too. It was a tragic loss for their family and friends, but I think they died as they had lived, unafraid.

There is strength for dying, as for living, that comes from being in control. Not the out-of-control desperation that leads physically healthy people to jump from bridges, but the in-control mechanism that says, "Here it is, death knocking at my door; I think I'll keep a hand on the knob."

Some people draw strength for their dying from a place, from a group of people, or a piece of music. Some find its direction through strong faith or wise teachings. Some use the force of their own personalities to bring to bear one or more of the above in what seems active participation in the process of their own dying.

However they approached their own death, the people whose stories are told in the chapters ahead showed ways to do it wisely, unafraid.

I think most of them found death no big bad thing.

A Sense of Place

When I first began to think seriously about dying, I didn't think *how* as much as *where*. You got sick, you went to the hospital, you died there. Or you got old, you went to a nursing home, you died there.

Then I began to change my mind about dying-places, and their implications.

By and large, hospitals and nursing homes are scary places. Useful to have around, if you are sick or old or in need of institutional care, but full of scary details: strange faces, acrid smells, unfamiliar sights and sounds, echoing corners empty of warmth. When I began to look closely at people who managed to die unafraid, I noticed they often died in places that offered just the opposite: familiar surroundings, comforting sights and sounds and smells.

What if it were possible to choose the latter when death approaches?

Some of us can, some can't. What slowly sunk into my head, as I began to notice people who faced death unafraid, was that attitudes and places seemed to react upon each other: the dying-place evoked fearlessness, the fearlessness infused the dying-place. In some dying-places, most notably hospitals and other institutions, surroundings of comfort—the elements that evoke fearlessness—are nearly impossible to create. That seems reason enough to seek ways of dying elsewhere whenever a choice can be made.

For most of us, there is a place representative of more than meets the eye: a backyard tree, a patch of land washed in colors of comfort, a kitchen fragrant with memories, a symphony hall or corner cafe or rooftop view. Sometimes, having been a best place on earth for life, a particular spot also becomes a place for taking leave— either by serendipitous accident or by design. And sometimes it is hard to tell which.

Take, for example, the case of a lady who walked into a private membership library in San Francisco some years back, laid her head on the table beside the books she had been reading, and quietly died. She had been a regular in that reading room, a place where book-lovers of all sorts come to escape from the whirling urban scene below.

When I asked later for details about the incident both the librarian and the board chairman, who happened to be an attorney, refused to discuss it, although nearly a decade had passed. It was as if something sinister had occurred on the premises, something unmentionable. As if the library might somehow be liable for ignoble participation in a perfectly natural occurrence, or the heirs might be traumatized by the reminder of a book lover's having died while surrounded by books.

Something seems absurd to me about the attitudes of these intelligent people. Would the family sue, all these years after the fact? Would the young clerk who discovered the dead woman be traumatized all over again? No, the library representatives' refusal to comment had to be grounded in the fine old American attitude toward death: Shhh, don't talk about it; that's far too personal, too intimate, unfit for discussion in polite society.

So the book lover remains anonymous. But I believe it is the library officials whose voices are fearful, not the woman who wordlessly died. I like to think that her last breaths might have been made easier by that particular happenstance of place.

For many of us at least, drawing a last breath over a good book in a favorite book-filled room does not seem at all a bad thing. Given the opportunity to choose, an opportunity that diminishes in direct proportion to the increase in extended-care facilities and nursing homes, wouldn't many of us select a similar favorite spot of our own for our own parting glance at this life?

Living, and dying, with a sense of place is both circumstance and gift. It is a gift when we find ourselves, somehow, in a place that lifts our spirits or fills us with comfort and "alrightness." As a circumstance, it is open to change.

Rick, the young man in a later chapter whose family helped in his battle to go home to die, won the change he sought. Others dying in hospitals and institutions, as a dismaying percentage of us do, substitute images that take them to places they cannot physically reach. A woman in an Atlanta hospital, an accomplished sailor, died not long ago while awaiting an organ transplant. In every available space in her small room there were photographs of nearby Lake Lanier. There was her graceful boat, seen from the dock as it glided toward a faraway island on a cloudless day. There were the quirky inlets of unexplored shoreline, the tangled hillsides rising abruptly to meet pine-covered mountains. There were expanses of azure water, acres of solitude on a winter morning. "My body may be here," she told the friends and family who would soon be scattering her ashes on those waters, "but my spirit is contentedly in that place."

The sailor chose, if only in her mind's eye, her place to be. Whether through imaging or in reality, making such a choice of place can go a long way toward helping one to die unafraid.

Sigurd Olson would unquestionably have chosen, as the place of his heart, the vast northern wilderness that centered his life. Olson was one of the foremost naturalists of the twentieth century, author of books and articles that chronicled his passion for wilderness, untamed waters and the creatures that dwell therein. He served as president of the Wilderness Society and the National Parks Association, as wilderness guide and protector throughout the U.S. and Canada, as consultant to the Department of the Interior and to countless conservation groups.

In his books, Olson wrote of " . . . an attachment to the land and a feeling for its antiquity," of an "intimate relationship with natural things close to me." Once he told of experiencing something he called "open horizons," a title he gave to one of his books. Writing of islands and headlands that, from a distance, can disappear into the horizon only to reappear hours or days later "as though I had passed through a door into the beyond itself," he theorized that life itself was a series of open horizons. The last such horizon, Olson said, would be that of "understanding the great imponderables."

Sigurd Olson, says his friend Kevin Proescholdt, head of Northern Minnesota's Friends of the Boundary Waters Wilderness, "had a sense and understanding of the natural rhythms and cycles of life."

In his later years, Olson suffered from Parkinson's disease. It interfered somewhat with his life, but did not keep him from either voyaging into the wilderness near his Minnesota home or from working regularly at the typewriter in his backyard "writing shack." He was at work on what would be his last book, *Of Time and Place*, published posthumously in 1982.

For Christmas 1981, their sons presented Sigurd and his wife Elizabeth with new sets of snowshoes. Soon afterwards Sig Olson laced his new snowshoes and headed into the white forests, the wilderness that was the place of his heart. He died that day, in that place, of sudden and unanticipated natural causes.

Before he left, Olson had rolled a new sheet of paper into his typewriter. On it were the words, "A new adventure is coming up, and I'm sure it will be a good one."

That final adventure of Sigurd Olson's began as had countless other adventures of the noted naturalist's long and productive life, with deliberate strides into the wilderness he loved. It was, from his earliest days on earth, a sacred place.

For Peter Fitzpatrick, the place of sacredness was not one of northern wilderness but of deep green open spaces. Peter's affection for the land was as lifelong as Sig Olson's, growing as it did from the sturdy Irish countryside of his birth. And though their earthly paths never crossed they would have understood each other's ties.

Although he came to the United States when he was young, grew up, married and raised a family in the American northeast, Peter Fitzpatrick's roots remained deep in the Irish soil, his most vivid memories framed within those scenes. One in particular was always at the forefront: the image of the day his beloved brother Larry left to work in the fields, but did not come home. Larry was found later, stretched out on his back on the lush green landscape where he had died, as if already returning to the good earth.

When Peter and his wife May moved to Florida after his retirement, they bought a patio home adjoining the fairway of a golf course where he regularly played three or four times a week. It was the fulfillment of a long-held dream, made sweeter by the fact that Peter's history of heart problems had made reaching retirement unlikely. He had twice undergone major heart surgery, each time disproving the predictions that he would never return to an active lifestyle.

One brilliant, crystal clear Florida morning Peter kissed his wife and walked out onto the fairway just after daybreak, carrying his driver. It was for him almost a ritual. On just about any clear day, before the course opened for play, Peter could be seen driving a few balls before breakfast. I knew that because I jogged around that same course in the early mornings, and occasionally waved to the diminutive golfer from the pathway.

This particular morning on an isolated, tree-lined part of the course Peter drove three passable shots down the fifteenth fairway, into the dawn. Then he stretched out on his back on the green grass, his golf club laid carefully beside him, his blue eyes gazing heavenward, and made his own private passage.

Out for an early-morning run, my husband and I rounded the bend moments after Peter's death. I remember thinking that this small, neatly dressed man seemed so at peace any interruption would somehow have been wrong. I don't believe it was simply my own sense of helplessness; there was a feeling of serenity around the two of us far stronger than any panicky sense of needing to revive him. I knelt beside him, held his hand and said strange things that came to my mind. I couldn't help talking to him. While my husband ran for help, I talked to this stranger about how peaceful he seemed, and how I thought he must be alright.

May Fitzpatrick and I, linked by this uncommon introduction, became good friends. In the days and months that followed she told me of Peter's background. "He loved living on the golf course," she said; "looking out across the green fairways into the trees. He used to say it reminded him of Ireland."

Two days after Peter died, I walked with May and their granddaughter around the back nine holes of the golf course, this time just before nightfall. They wanted to see the spot where he had last lain, to look down the fairway where those three balls had fallen. "It does look peaceful," said May. "You can't see houses, or anything but green from here. I think Peter must have rested easy."

May believes the expression on Peter's dead face portrayed an authentic sense of peace. She stops short of thinking he set out to die; she simply feels there was somehow a rightness to it all, an appropriateness of place.

Her husband, May recalls, was strongly affected by the manner of his older brother's death. Larry had been the eldest of six Fitzpatrick siblings, with Peter the youngest. Peter, who retained a brogue and manner redolent of the Emerald Isle, named his own son Larry, a new link with generations to come. And the old mind-portrait of his brother in death on the Irish soil, May says, was one of Peter's strongest links to generations past. Looking down the lush, green fairway into the forested scene that had been his parting mortal glimpse, she felt he must have had a sense of connectedness.

No one knows what spacial connections there are to be made after the dying process is completed. Perhaps there *is* some heavenly site, gold-paved streets and all, or a spot that equals in beauty the northern wilderness or southern meadow. But whatever later links are made, there seems a connection between places of the mortal heart and the process of dying unafraid.

There was an intriguing story, not long ago, of a man named John Earl James, who lived and died in Oakland, California. It is likely that the only headlines he ever generated were those that appeared over the stories published soon after his death. I was among those caught up in the saga as reported in the *Oakland Tribune* and *The San Francisco Chronicle*. My curiosity led me to speak later with James' brother about the details and ask permission to include his story here.

John Earl James, who was born in 1940, spent his childhood in a gabled, two-story Victorian house on Willow Street in Oakland, with a yard that was the largest in the neighborhood. Nearby were historic homes of some of the city's most prominent citizens. There were sidewalks and shade trees and there was the sense of childhood well-being that permeated many communities of the time.

James grew up, married, had three children, and worked as a machinist until his retirement. But he suffered from a form of asthma so severe that one attack, family members said later, eventually affected his brain. He began to suffer from a form of dementia somewhat akin to Alzheimer's.

During the last few years of his life James lived at a board-and-care facility far across the city from Willow Street. He seldom strayed from its grounds, though he would talk of "going back home to my dad." Family members would visit, gently reminding him that his father had died years earlier, and trying to offer reassurance. No one, though, talked much about the old home place. It had long ago been sold, fallen into disrepair and suffered the peculiar afflictions that vandals, wine-drinking passersby and rainfall through rooftop holes can bring. Its windows had long been boarded over, and weeds had claimed the play-yard.

John Earl James disappeared one day, after being treated and released at a local hospital for an asthma attack. Family and caregivers searched a wide area, but could turn up no trace of the missing man. They knew that when he left the hospital James was still wearing slippers and a wrist identification bracelet. They also knew there were miles of traffic-congested streets around, where mishap might be expected and where passage for even the most self-assured pedestrian can be a challenge.

Weeks later, a man walking his dog in the old neighborhood discovered the body of John Earl James, lying amid the detritus of what had been the refuge of his youth, the house on Willow Street. He had managed to get home for his final passage.

For another Californian, Marion Young, "home" had often been associated with seagoing vessels. A long affection for ships and the sea began, for Young, with World War II Navy service that won him seven battle stars and included membership in the task force that launched Jimmy Doolittle's air raid on Tokyo in 1942. Among the ships he survived was the destroyer *Monson*, torpedoed by the Japanese with Young on board. Memories of the *Monson* and other offshore homes stayed with him.

Young had a long career as a business executive, keeping the ties to his Navy background through membership, and an eventual vice-commander spot, in the American Legion Post in San Francisco. He cared for his wife during a four-year illness that preceded her death in 1991, but according to his son Dennis, Young often said his choice would be to die of a sudden massive heart attack as had his two brothers.

One of Young's retirement interests centered around the *SS Jeremiah O'Brien*, a World War II Liberty Ship which was one of more than 2700 identically designed cargo vessels produced by U.S. shipyards between March 1941 and November

1945. The *O'Brien* fared better than the *Monson*. Thanks largely to the efforts of a non-profit corporation formed in 1978 the *O'Brien* was restored, became a National Monument and was listed by the National Trust for Historic Preservation. She eventually became a permanent part of the San Francisco waterfront scene, open to visitors and for volunteer restoration work that continues to keep the *O'Brien* seaworthy. Seaworthy enough, it turned out, to make the long journey from the Golden Gate through the Panama Canal and across the Atlantic to Normandy for the 50th anniversary of D-Day in June 1994.

For Christmas 1993, Dennis and his wife gave Marion Young a membership in the *Jeremiah O'Brien*, and from then on the old ship was a focal point of his life. Young was not able to go to Normandy, but he served as a regular volunteer and as assistant manager of the ship's store. In the summer of 1996 he made a nine-week voyage to the Pacific Northwest with others of the *O'Brien's* crew.

Shortly after the *O'Brien* returned to San Francisco from that voyage, Young and some of his friends had a party on board. "There were always people on board," Dennis Young says, "mostly old Navy or Merchant Marine men. That night he was with people he loved, doing what he most wanted to do." His friends said Young was in good spirits.

While the party was underway, Young was walking from one part of the ship to another. He paused in a doorway, and without warning pitched forward, victim of a massive heart attack. Later, the family had a memorial on board the *O'Brien*, tossing a wreath at the close of the service onto the waters of San Francisco Bay.

Just as many a reader is most at home while holding a book, many an artist knows peace with a paintbrush in hand. The Social Realist artist Moses Soyer went to the Hamptons for Labor Day weekend in 1974 but cut his trip short and returned to New York and his tenth floor Chelsea Hotel studio to work. He wanted to finish a painting for possible inclusion in a retrospective of his work scheduled to open October 15.

During Soyer's long career his model was often a dancer, as his late wife had been. This time it was the dancer Phoebe Neville, who had often posed for him. At one point Soyer told Neville it was time for her to take a rest break, while he sat in his chair to study the work in progress. When she returned he was still seated, facing the easel, dead of a massive heart attack.

Places, it would seem, may in some sense ease one's passage. The Aztecs had a notion of this in their concept of the place where infants and very young children go, which they called "chichihuacuauhco." It is a combination of the words for wet-nurse (chichihua), tree (cuahitl) and place (co); the Aztecs saw it as a place where the children are nourished by milk that falls in drops from the tree.

Stonewall Jackson may have had another, but similarly comforting, scene in mind when he spoke what were reported to be his dying words. "Let us cross over the river," said the embattled soldier, "and rest under the shade of the trees." A reassuring thought, midway into a grisly battle.

Places—trees, fields, houses, sandy beaches or particular rooms—have always been part of our coming to terms with dying. Religions offer the halls of our ancestors, or pictures of a cloud-bordered heaven, or perhaps the promise of a better place in another world. People of all persuasions, when facing death, often call upon the images of life that represent touchstones to the best places life has offered. And for many who seem to die unafraid that significant space is brought a little closer, the touchstone becoming a useful part of the experience. A final place of the heart.

Making Peace

There is a common denominator hard to overlook in stories of those who die unafraid. It is the experience of making peace. The cornerstone of most great religions, peacemaking has long been acknowledged to have a lot to do with successful living; it may have just as much to do with fearless dying. Several stories I have encountered seem remarkable for the very different ways in which they illustrate this theory.

The general idea of making peace before dying, in order to die in peace, has been around since the origin of good ideas; it remains a fairly common custom in many cultures. Usually it involves mending broken relationships, accepting responsibility for past mistakes, apologizing for old wounds one may have inflicted on another. The big problem with putting these sorts of things off until the last minute, of course, is that the denial of death can take up so much time and energy it is suddenly too late to scurry around tidying up messes.

Lillian Ding and Aline Appel were two who tidied up. Neither Lillian nor Aline knew of the other's existence, but these two starkly different women living in vastly different worlds shared an almost mystical perception of their own dying. For them, the immediacy of probable death prompted personal transformations that wove new and interesting threads into the fabric of their lives. Making peace became part of their way of dying unafraid.

I knew Lillian, whose husband had been a family friend for many years, only in the years of her dying. She was gracious in sharing those years with me, as well as with others who were dying themselves. Aline I came to know after her death, through her daughter's stories and her own end-of-life poetry.

Lillian Ding, going about the business of dying, could be as radiantly alive as anyone I have known. Her luminescence was enough to make one curious.

When we first met, in the early 1990s, I thought Lillian was just an extremely pretty Chinese woman whose quiet, almost deferential air seemed contradictory to what was indeed fact: that she was a skilled, internationally respected physician, mother of four high-achieving children and recently a grandmother. The grandmother part was made even more baffling by the fact that her face, at sixty-something, was the face of a thirty year-old. Lillian's utterly serene expression sometimes gave me the impression that she was enjoying, deep inside, a private little joke. And this may have been true. She did know that at sixty she looked more like thirty or forty. She also knew that while dying she could communicate a remarkable sense of vibrancy.

"You know, Lillian," I said once, "you ought to try looking worse, so maybe you'd get a little more sympathy."

"Oh, well, then," she said, in her lilting Chinese-accented English, "and what good would it be? Maybe it's better I keep on looking well; that way I think I don't see so many worried faces around me." She laughed at her own philosophical response.

Lillian was born in pre-revolutionary Canton, China, the daughter of a wealthy physician whose rigid Christianity apparently overlooked the part about love and compassion. She spent a good bit of her childhood and youth in a vain search for some nugget of paternal approbation. The bad news of that effort was that in their relationship her father never softened; the good news was that her enormous struggle to prove herself got her through college and rigorous medical training in America at a time (the 1940s and 50s) when such a career path was not easy even for U.S.-born women.

After finishing her medical training, Lillian married another physician of Chinese descent, Borneo-born Lik Kiu Ding. The two of them, devout Christians in spite of her father's somewhat discouraging example, went to Sarawa to start that area's first hospital under the auspices of the Methodist church. Four adventurous years later they moved to Hong Kong, where they practiced and raised their family.

By her own account, Lillian was a perfectionist who demanded perfection of others. She was also an accomplished worrier, either about small details that failed to meet her expectations or about vast, nebulous issues like what might happen after Hong Kong was returned to Chinese control in 1997. For years she was desperate to immigrate and her husband was adamant about staying. "I cried every night," she said of that great fear, "and prayed to God that I wanted to die."

In early 1987 it seemed that prayer was about to be answered. Lillian was found to have stage two cancer, which meant, she explained later, "the outlook was not so good." She spent ten days in the hospital in Hong Kong undergoing surgery to remove one breast and having a dissection of her axillary lymph nodes which revealed the extent of her cancer. In her spare time, she read up on the medications she was taking, confirming the fact that they could not cure her, only perhaps buy a little time.

It was at this point that Lillian Ding made the first move toward what would prove to be an extended, but often remarkable, process of dying. Finding herself depressed over the state of her health she made a sort of mental about-face. She developed a way of counting her blessings which had the effect of becoming an ongoing relaxation technique.

She also developed a pain-control mechanism not unlike the mantras used in civilizations past and by others whose stories appear in these pages. Lillian's particular tool was to repeat the twenty-third psalm.

"As a matter of fact," she recalled later about that period, "to have this operation *is* painful. Particularly in my right arm where there was swelling and it was very tender, every time I rolled over it was like a knife stabbing me. But somehow, when I have pain, I just recite the twenty-third psalm, and I know that He will walk with me through the valley of the shadow of death, and I shall not fear . . . "

After the hospital stay Lillian went home feeling rested and at peace. "I remember," she said later, "that it was during the Chinese New Year. The weather was beautiful and sunny, and my husband took me out to the New Territory every day. We would just go into the countryside and sit in the sunshine, just rest and talk. We really had a very good time."

The "very good time" did not, however, change the fact that Lillian could expect a local recurrence of her cancer to grow on skin and scar tissue and be very difficult to treat. Lik Kiu's nephew in California, a radiotherapist, urged them to come to America for a six-week radiotherapy treatment to decrease her chances of local recurrence. In mid-February they made the long trip across the Pacific.

The radiotherapy was followed by a dangerous drop in Lillian's white blood cell count and, later, by an extremely painful bout with what was called "a frozen shoulder." Not even the twenty-third psalm seemed to help the shoulder pain. "Some mornings (when) I could not sleep," she recalled, "I would say, 'God, I'm not afraid of dying, but how long is this pain to last?'." God made no immediate response. But the questioner did outlast the pain. After getting back to Hong Kong and months of physiotherapy there, the shoulder slowly thawed. That episode was followed by additional problems, though, which eventually brought Lillian and Lik Kiu back to California to stay.

And despite the odds and her avowed fearlessness, Lillian Ding did not die that year, or the next, or the next. What she did instead was turn the fact of her dying, which would happen on January 2, 1997, into a remarkably transformed living. Her death came precisely ten years to the day after the first sign of her cancer.

Lillian, who had no wish to die, packed the extra days she fought for with activity. She racked up an impressive list of postoperative achievements, including hospice work in Hong Kong and the founding of the first Chinese-language cancer support group in her California community. She had a growing family scattered around the globe, of which she was inordinately proud. What was curious, to the outside observer, was the delight she seemed to take in the dying process, and in communicating the sense that although death might be winning the game, she was playing her last hand very well.

"It's very freeing," she told me about a year before she died. She had been talking of giving away her possessions, and of how this was a way of unburdening herself. "My niece, when I gave her a piece of very expensive jewelry, said, 'Oh, you must keep this for yourself, and wear it as long as you can.' But I told her, 'If I leave it to you when I die it has no value; but if I give it to you now, it still has value.'

"And if someone is unkind," she went on, in her explanation of this new freedom, "if I pass someone on the street who is rude to me, well, you know, I can just say, 'Well, the hell with you, I'm *dying*.'" Lillian's disdain for pretense and piety was a fascinating part of how she played the hand well.

In October, 1994, as part of a support-therapy group process, Lillian wrote a letter to Cancer and Cancer's reply.

"Dear Cancer," the first letter begins

> You have been with me since 1987. When you
> came into my life, it was the turning point—thanks
> to God's mercy—from despair to hope . . .

She goes on to talk about how she had always felt herself to be happy and successful but in retrospect believes that was only on the surface. The real happiness, she confides to Cancer, came from learning to let her children go and from resolving misunderstandings with her sisters, after she faced her own mortality.

> . . . I learned to accept death as part of life's journey—
> but not the end. When one conquers death, one is
> not afraid any more.

And she gives a hint about how much she is enjoying herself:

> I have to thank you, Cancer, since you entered my life.
> These are the most productive and satisfying years of my
> life. People ask me why I look younger and more beau-
> tiful. I tell them that because of your challenge I am
> younger in spirit, maybe not in body.

Lillian winds up her letter with a philosophy lecture to Cancer:

> Life is like a mirror. Others look at you and they respond
> with your reflection. When I change to be more com-
> passionate, forgiving and loving, the people around me
> also change with me.
>
> So, Cancer, you may work very hard on me. You
> may destroy my body, but not my soul and spirit.

She ends by likening Cancer to a grain of sand that got into her, but which she coated with love and kindness,

> . . . transforming you into a beautiful South Sea pearl. Even after I die, it will shine in the darkness, to help some people who lost heart to regain their faiths.

Cancer, in its response to Lillian, didn't appreciate this last at all, or much of the rest of her two-page letter.

> "Dear Lillian," Cancer writes back
>
> I was surprised and amused when I got your letter . . . We have had several encounters, (and) in the end you always got ahead of me. You should know by now that most of these conventional therapies only pushed me into a corner. Eventually, I would be back...
>
> . . . Then you gathered your strength and founded a cancer support group in Hong Kong. You even called each other 'cancer friends.' What an insult! Last of all, I don't want to be a South Sea pearl. I don't care how beautifully you described it. I don't want to be entombed in loving kindness forever.
>
> Sincerely yours,
> Cancer

Lillian's fanciful tilting with death—or Cancer—would continue, along with her unabashed enjoyment of the freedom that fearlessness brought. Cancer would eventually win, but no one could see Lillian as having lost.

Aline Wharton Appel was as committed to an enlightened agnosticism as Lillian Ding was to Christianity. But Aline might have written a similar letter to Cancer in the scant six weeks which she had between diagnosis and death. She wrote, instead, several poems that express both her own fearlessness and an about-face (for Aline) search for earthly reconciliation. Beyond reconciliation and death Aline saw not heaven but a sort of magical continuity of which she would become a logical part. Death, the interim point, became OK, a gentle vessel into which she decided to pour herself.

Aline Appel grew up in Washington, D.C. at about the same time that Lillian Ding was growing up in Canton and Hong Kong. Their similarities end there. Aline married, had two children, and spent her adult life "in a constant battle with herself," according to her daughter Stacy.

"She was a very creative artist who didn't believe in her own skills and abilities," Stacy says. "She had friends, equally creative and intelligent, who were also ill suited to the 'D.C. housewife' mold of those years. Most of them had a crutch: food, shopping, alcohol. Always you knew not to call after five."

In early 1986 Aline and her husband were putting the finishing decorative touches, via long distance phone calls, on a new house they had bought and redesigned near the California coast, when she was diagnosed with a fast-growing cancer that would kill her in a matter of weeks.

Midway through treatment in Washington, Aline opted to stage a festive, farewell-for-California exit. While her son on the West Coast filled the new house with rented furniture and household necessities, Aline spent her last days on the East Coast saying cheerful goodbyes to friends she knew she would not see again.

Disguising the severity of her illness behind a smile, Aline boarded a regular commercial flight with her husband and daughter. It turned into an elegant cross-country journey, with champagne toasts making a celebration out of what might easily have been a time for tears.

In her remaining weeks Aline set about making peace with her family, the son and daughter from whom she had kept herself walled off to varying extents and the husband who had known her bitterness. Often using metaphors from the California scenery that framed her final days, she talked of openness and richness, energy and colors. And when the headaches from a brain tumor became acute, she talked to Stacy (whose career included work for a California hospice) about her fears and regrets.

"She asked once," Stacy recalls, "if I thought dying would be painful. I said that what my experience with lung cancer patients suggested was that she would eventually slip into a sleepy kind of coma and would not experience pain at the end."

Weeks before she died, Aline wrote a poem entitled "Rich Lode:"

A striking! A strike indeed!
I have been mining through the night
Panning the golden ore in a gentle river by my side
Hastening to wash it pure and sweet.

Unending vein—
and suddenly replenished
now in my heart these riches, safe forever:

he who fathered son, daughter, all dear loves, oh
rich! rich! rich! Where can I spend it all
    to set the world aright? so much love
    unending beauty! I'm a robber baron
    capturing all the world! How can I set it right
    with all this wealth? . . . I know! A secret
map where bounty can be hidden.
                                    —A. Appel, 1986

Aline became gradually comatose over a period of days.
She died peacefully one brilliant California morning, with her
family at her side.

Did Lillian and Aline follow some secret map into their
singularly fearless deaths? I think so. Maps of their own making, charts worthy of study by the living. Born into totally different cultures and raised in vastly different circumstances,
these two women of the twentieth century left a timeless message about the unfeared death.

Stories of deathbed confessions and absolutions, followed
by a sense of tranquility that seemed to evidence itself in the
dying person, abound in history and literature as well as in family lores. The Knights of the Roundtable made ritualized
farewells. Apologies for real or imagined wrongdoings are tra-
ditionally included in end-of-life statements, contemporary
prisoners often focus on a search for earthly reconciliation
when facing death. Lillian Ding and Aline Appel simply added
some clear and personal roadmaps for this common journey.

Two starkly differing stories I witnessed not long ago in
a southern nursing home reinforce my belief in the value of
earthly reconciliation as a pathway toward fearless dying.

Miranda, who lay shriveled and moaning as she clung tenaciously to life, had two daughters in their forties. Each lived more than 600 miles distant, each came to see her every few months, and each seemed to have a thinly veiled dislike for Miranda, a sentiment she returned. "Disappointment" was the word she often used about them, although their worldly achievements at least would have made most mothers proud. It was as if their strongest connections were through some bond of obstinate anger. I did not like to be in the room when the daughters visited.

But Miranda had been my friend in happier days, when she was a fiercely independent, competent businesswoman. I continued to visit her as she deteriorated to a terrible physical depth, and tried to reconcile my own conflictions of guilt and piousness as I prayed for her to die.

In Miranda's room there were no pictures. There were only white walls, white sheets and blankets pulled smoothly against her gray face. I would sometimes bring a sprig of impatiens blossoms in a paper cup to put on her bedside tray, but it was hard to challenge the bleak colorlessness of that room.

Over a period of about sixteen months, during which I listened to dozens of small-talk family conversations, a typical exchange between Miranda and a visiting daughter would be:

Miranda: Oh, it's you. When did you come?
Daughter: Last night. The plane was oversold and late; it was an awful trip. How're you doing?
M: About as well as you could expect, in this place.

D: Now, Mama, you know it's the best nursing home in the county. And you're going to get the best possible care, no matter what it costs.

M: I'd be better off dead.

D: Oh, Mama, don't say that. We need you.

I don't know what those conversations were about. We had no psychiatrist friends in common who might have figured it out, or perhaps have brought about some kindness on one side or another. All I know is that the bitterness in that little family lingered just as Miranda lingered—and that her daughters would nevertheless end every conversation with those words: "We need you."

Almost directly across the hall from Miranda's room in the nursing home was a relatively young man, victim of some malady that had left him paralyzed and unable to talk except in heavily slurred phrases. He had been, I was told, a fairly successful businessman, largely because he was a tyrant. A well-off tyrant, with a lot of clients but no excess of friends and admirers. Apparently the best thing he had going for him was a business partner named Charlie. I never met Charlie. I came to admire him, during the months we were visiting friends in nearby rooms, solely on the basis on what I overheard when visiting Miranda across the hall and what the nurses told me.

Charlie would come to see Norman the Tyrant, and I would hear their conversations at the end of the hall, where Norman spent most of his days secured to a wheelchair beside the picture window. A typical conversation between the two of *them* would go something like this:

C: How's it going, big guy?

N: C-cd be better.

C: Well, things could be better around the office, too, if we could get you back. But you left everything in pretty good shape so it rocks along.

N: Yehh?

C: Yeah. Walter came by. Asked about you. Said you were a hard-nosed S.O.B. but you sure knew the business. Know what, Norm? I think he loves you.

N: Yehh? Tell Walter, 'm sorry.

I never knew what Norman was sorry about. But I heard similar exchanges over and over. Charlie would mention someone, Norman would say, "Tell him 'm sorry." Or "Tell him, 'e's OK." And each time, Norman would seem to relax a little more.

Miranda's daughters came less and less often, as she became less and less communicative. Her last months were in and out of comas. I would sometimes just rub her forehead and feel sad, trying to remember what she looked like when she smiled. Like her daughters, I would find excuses not to go to see this shriveled shell of the person I had known; or I would stop for an embarrassingly brief moment at Miranda's bedside, often smiling at Norman or Charlie as I passed.

One day, about three or four months after I first noticed Norman in the hallway, another nameplate appeared on his door. I asked the nurse where he had gone.

"Norman?" she said; "oh, Norman died. Unexpectedly, because he was still physically strong. But there was no chance he was going to get better. You know, he had no family at all, but that friend of his had been by just that morning."

I do not know about Miranda, who died before the end of her second year in that place where she never wanted to be. I hope she found the peace that seemed so elusive all those months. Just on the basis of those enigmatic conversations I overheard, I believe Norman died, like Lillian and Aline, after final days of reconciliation rather than bitterness. What the three of them shared was an inborn suggestion that is part of the human life-experience, a voice that says, "Wouldn't it be a good idea to try to make peace?"

For Lillian Ding, making peace became not just a way of living but a way of dying. In Aline Appel's case it came with an exuberant reach into the unknown, an excitement over the discovery of how reconciliation could enhance her living and dying alike.

Norman's peace-making may be simply a figment of my imagination, but I don't think so. His earnestness with those repeated extensions of olive branches was so clear, I believe some of the peace that may have eluded him earlier was captured, finally, in his dying months.

What the three of them left behind are roadmaps, clues for the living about dying unafraid.

A Moment in Time

There's something to be said for markers. Anniversary dates, graduations, notches on trees to etch significant moments into history, these and countless other rituals serve as pegs on which to hang our lifespans. Ways of holding onto the past or reaching into the future. As a child, I was fond of stringing connected paper dolls around the walls of my room, counted out precisely according to the days remaining until some glorious event was to occur. I would carefully tear off one paper doll each morning and, at the end, there would be a star to paste on the calendar.

Other markers function somewhat like bargaining chips with oneself or someone else or God. "If I finish this project, I'll take a whole day off" or, "Just get me through this experience, and the next will be manageable" or "Please, help me through this recovery program and I'll quit smoking afterwards."

The day of one's dying will eventually paste itself onto the calendar whether one wishes it to or not. A final notch, ultimate graduation. What is worth noticing is the way that some people, walking the path toward their dying moment, set their own markers.

Vee Huie was such a traveler. A friend and neighbor throughout the time our children were growing up together, Vee was married in the 1950s and member of one of the last generations in which stay-at-home wives and mothers were common. She reveled in that job. Vee took enormous pride and delight in her Columbia Presbyterian Seminary professor husband, Wade, and the four high-achieving sons they produced over the next decade.

Her friends used to joke about having a sort of love/hate relationship with Vee. Her desserts were always perfect, her sons were invariably president of everything, her multitudinous tasks invariably well done and her opinions too often right; but she was a kind, generous and unfailingly loyal friend. So it was hard not to rejoice with her, and easy to laugh with her. As her sons married and grandsons began to appear, Vee had only one major, unfulfilled wish: she wanted a granddaughter.

When she was diagnosed with cancer while barely into her fifties Vee battled back with characteristic vehemence and grace. Over a period of years, she won many of those battles. She underwent repeated therapies, often emerging with surprising strength, and in March 1992, years past her initial diagnosis, joined her husband on a joyous trip to Jamaica. The following month her cancer reappeared, this time in the colon. Despite the long odds, she began chemotherapy once again and stuck with it until August. It was then that Vee, her family and doctors faced the fact that nothing further could be done.

Told they could expect another two to three months at most, Vee and Wade called their son David, who was then living in Australia. David moved up his plans for a Christmas visit home, and came several weeks after the call instead. He brought his wife Miriam and the news that they were expecting a daughter the next year—who would be named Nicole Vee Huie. Wade recalls those days, during which the rest of the family came for long conversations, extensive picture-taking, and saying good-bye, as "a bitter-sweet experience." No one expected Vee to live past Thanksgiving.

But Thanksgiving became only a marker. "The baby was due in early March," Wade wrote later to a friend, "and Vee kept saying she was going to hang on until that baby got here. That 'dream' seemed to me to be the only unrealistic part of her approach to her death, though I never said so. In the light of the two or three months suggestion (the previous August) from the doctor I thought Vee was really pushing it to hope for March."

At Christmas, Vee was still able to travel to a nearby state for a holiday visit with another son, but early in the new year she began a downward slide. Still she clung tenaciously to life, and to the burning wish to stay on this earth until her namesake arrived to mark, in a sense, her grandmother's place. As she was slipping into unconsciousness on February 19 a call came from the delivery room of a hospital in Melbourne, Australia, with the news from David that Nicole Vee had indeed entered the world. A friend in the room, who was also a nurse, asked Vee to blink her eyes if she understood her granddaughter had arrived; when she responded, it was a final gesture. Several hours later, Vee died.

I had not seen Vee since shortly after the last recurrence of her cancer. I went by to model the dress I'd bought for my coming wedding and introduce the prospective bridegroom, two things she said she wanted to approve. During that visit, though, we had talked about what she saw as the extraordinary goodness of her life, and the mixed feelings she had about its end. Possessed of a deep, carefully studied Christian faith, she said she had no fears about where she was going and only gratitude for where she had been. "But I *am mad*," she said, "that I won't see (youngest son and later a minister) Scott graduate, or see my grandchildren grow up . . . " She didn't know, then, about Nicole Vee, or I'm certain she would have been maddest about missing the baby's birth. I think when she got that news, waiting for her granddaughter became a final determination, a final marker.

In his excellent book *Death as a Fact of Life*, David Hendin points out that dying days and weeks often bear direct relationships to significant events. Such events might be a part of the bargaining phase that is midway through the generally acknowledged stages of the dying process (denial, anger, bargaining, depression, acceptance, as first outlined by Elizabeth Kubler-Ross) or be related to a sort of bouyancy surrounding celebratory occasions. Hendin cites studies showing that people tend to "hold onto life until after a birthday, an election, a religious holiday, or another event to which they look forward," and anecdotal material further supporting this theory. Two such events frequently cited, which Hendin also notes, are the deaths of both John Adams and Thomas Jefferson on the Fourth of July, fifty years after the signing of the Declaration of Independence.

Vee Huie was both strong bargainer and celebrant. While she was declaring to friends and family her intention of hanging on until the new granddaughter arrived, I think she used that marker as both a bargaining chip and a prize, a way to live out her life a winner even in dying.

Another woman of determination was Ming Levinson. Raised in the jungles of Bolivia and Peru where her father was a mining engineer in the 1930s, Ming, says her widower Tom Rose, "was somebody who really grabbed onto life." When the two met she had just turned fifty and had decided to revisit the places she had lived. To accomplish this Ming had planned a long, overland journey using only trains, buses and cars.

"We were smitten," Tom recalls. "I said, 'I'll meet you in Guatemala,' and I did, and we had ten days. I said, 'I'll meet you in Peru . . . '" Some meetings later they came back to the U.S. and Mill Valley, California.

Ming was a primal therapist with a degree in psychiatry, and training in meditation and other paths to self-understanding. She had had cancer in her thirties, an almost benign form of lymphoma. When, several years after she and Tom met, it returned as an aggressive, large-cell lymphoma, her response was to sit down and make a list of all of the potential therapies available. The list ran to two pages.

"She went through the list and crossed out the ones she didn't feel comfortable with," Tom says, "and then set about the others." They carried her through for a time, seemingly strong and in good spirits, until an unexpected setback landed her in the hospital where it was soon clear she would not pull through.

"She wanted everyone who had been in her life to be around her," Tom says of those final days. "So they came: her friends came, her children came, the woman who had introduced us came. She was able to be present with them all."

But one person was missing. Lloyd, a man Ming had lived with for ten years, "was closer to her than I," Tom says. "He was sort of a spiritual soulmate." Ming, by now clearly dying, wanted Lloyd in on this part of her life cycle, but he was miles away in Oregon.

When Tom called and told him to come, Lloyd said, "Well, but I've got to get my car fixed." "I said, 'Lloyd, you'd better rent a car'." Finally he called to say he was on his way. Lloyd and Tom sat by the bedside for four or five hours, until Ming left on her final journey.

Tom Rose had had an earlier experience that supports his belief in the usefulness of markers for the dying. Just as he finished high school his mother was diagnosed with a badly metasticized and particularly vicious stomach cancer, which doctors said would end her life within a matter of days. She said No, that she intended to see her son off to college. "In September I left for college," he says, "and two weeks later she died."

The two experiences at widely separated times of his life left Tom with no less a sense of loss—but with a conviction that there is something within each of us, a hidden strength, a spiritual connection that may be available to help us touch the markers we reach for as life is ending.

Grace, a California mother of nine, made a determined reach for several such markers. Grace was diagnosed with pancreatic cancer in mid-October of 1993, and told she could not expect to live very long. According to her daughter Missy, Grace set herself three goals: to attend the January wedding of her youngest son, to have a vacation trip to San Francisco with her husband later that month, and to live until her forty-fifth wedding anniversary on February 22, 1994.

Missy was a middle child of the nine. "I was Number 4 and my twin brother Number 5," she says. "When Mom found she was having twins she thought of us as double blessings from God. After her next four pregnancies, she asked for no more blessings." A tenth child, a girl born between Number 3 and the twins, had lived only three days.

Grace's husband and children were understandably the focus of her life. She did get to her son's wedding, "looking beautiful in spite of being sick," and she did take the trip to San Francisco for a memorable good time. But as her wedding anniversary date approached she was in a rapid decline. Several times on February 21 she raised her hand and said, looking off into space, "Let's go." As the gathered children watched and listened, it became clear to them that the one their mother was reaching for was the baby girl who had not lived to be there.

Something else, though, was still on Grace's mind. "She kept asking, 'What time is it?'" Missy says; "and we knew it was the anniversary that was so important to her." At ten in the morning of February 22, her wedding date, Grace died.

What may have been a record for pushing death's timing was reported in a story that ran on Christmas Day of 1994 in

The Virginian-Pilot and the Ledger-Star. The story concerned a 75-year-old man named Jim Schaeffer who had been taken to the hospital in Reston, Virginia a month earlier after collapsing at church. He was declared dead at 12:46 p.m. that day, the cause of death listed as heart disease and stroke.

But Schaeffer's wife begged him to hang on until their son and daughter could get to the hospital, and then made a call to his close friend and pastor, Philip Williams. Williams, arriving after Schaeffer's heart monitor had gone flat, touched his friend and said a prayer. Hospital personnel were preparing to remove the body when they noticed the monitor showed a heartbeat, and blood was charted again flowing in his veins.

Eventually, Schaeffer rallied to tell his friends and family he loved them, ask that God bless them—and ask for his son Philip. It was ninety minutes after he first revived that Philip walked in the door to hug his father, and Jim Schaeffer closed his eyes for the final time.

Was Jim Schaeffer in fact dead the first time he was pronounced so? Would Grace have died a few days earlier if she hadn't been waiting for her anniversary or a few days later if the anniversary had fallen on February 27? No one will know in this lifetime. What we do know is that these markers had had meaning for the living, and had given additional meaning to the dying. Maybe the message is simply to pay more attention to the times and people we cherish before our own dying is upon us.

Listening to the Nightsong

In more primitive cultures, simpler times, we humans lived closer to the earth—planting crops according to cycles of the moon, watching the rhythm of the tides, keeping a careful balance with the seasons. Some of it was due to mystical reasoning, but being closely attuned to nature was also a matter of practical survival: if you didn't take notice of the approaching storm it might very well wash you away.

Dying, in more primitive cultures and simpler times, may have been made simpler itself for the same reasons. Not that pain and anguish were any less, or grieving easier, or dying itself any more acceptable. But paying attention to the cycles of nature and rhythms of the earth has always been a valuable way of recognizing the cycle of life when it is closing. Today's technology enables us to have immense control over nature, whether we use that control wisely or not. But I tend to agree with the bumper sticker sent by a friend who lives gently in a remote area of Northern California, directly above the intersection of three major fault lines. It says: *Nature Bats Last.*

My grandmother knew that. Grandmother's entire life was spent on farms, mostly farms just big enough to provide eggs and milk for the family along with whatever fruits and vegetables could be coaxed from the Virginia soil. Sunday dinner at Grandmother's was, before it reached the table, a work of nature in progress. It involved rounding up a couple of likely chickens to fry, lopping off their heads with the axe or, worse, holding one in each hand and swinging them quickly in wide arcs. Grandmother did this routinely, not I. I never worked up nerve enough to try. But I learned first hand the meaning of "running around like a chicken with its head cut off."

I also first learned about newborn kittens and calves and pigs on my Uncle Porter's farm where Grandmother lived out her final years. Birth and death, like the whims of nature that could flood the crops with a summer rain or produce a lightning bolt capable reducing the barn to ashes, were part of Grandmother's daily existence. She buried countless friends and relatives, and regularly held hands with the sick and dying of her rural preacher husband's flock.

I don't think Grandmother died particularly "well", though she would certainly disapprove of my making such an assertion. During the time when she lay dying on a makeshift bed in our downstairs library, what I recall most is coming home from third grade bursting with plans for climbing trees with my friends and having to go first to pay a visit to Grandmother's room. There I would be questioned about whether I'd done my homework and helped Mother, and I would always, always, receive a few words about how ready Grandmother was to die and "be with your Grandfather." I heard those words to mean that if I were a little better perhaps Grandmother would not be so ready to clear out of there. Old-fashioned Protestant guilt in immense doses.

But whether or not she truly welcomed the event, I'm certain that Grandmother had no particular fear of dying simply because it was her familiar. Like birthing animals and respecting nature, dying was part of life. Even the more urban citizens of Grandmother's day had familiarities of the same sort. Nature's rhythms and cycles were a part of daily life and dying, the final progression of those rhythms, was accepted as being just what it is: part of the cycle. Today's urban living allows most of us very little contact with such cycles.

The sense of awe that can put human existence into perspective when one gazes up from the floor of Yosemite Valley or out from the top of a roaring waterfall is, more often than not, a vacation-time experience rather than part of our daily lives—so it is easy to miss the clues about lifespans and mortality that nature so gracefully provides.

Some leading naturalists of the recent past, though, along with hundreds of ordinary people who lived close to the earth, have left clues about how their philosophy of living played a significant role in their dying. Sigurd Olson, striding off into the woods he loved on a new pair of snowshoes, Rachel Carson making final contact with the sea and the gardens she had spent her life protecting, seemed focused on a world well known while headed toward a new place.

Years ago in Decatur, Georgia, an elderly man was dying of lung disease. He had made his living as a handyman/gardener. It could not have been an easy life, but he talked about those years of hard labor as if they had been sheer joy. His wife had died some time earlier, though, and with no one left to look after him he had moved, finally and unhappily, to the county nursing home.

His first name was Marshall, but because there was a younger man there who happened to have the last name of Marshall, the newcomer quickly became Old Marsh. Old Marsh didn't mind his new name or his new surroundings particularly, but from the day he arrived it was clear he would have preferred to be elsewhere. And he was simply tired of this old earth. "All my people are gone," he used to say. "I want to go be with my people."

Old Marsh had a constitution that seemed, though, not ready to let his soul go be with his people. Except for his failing lungs, he still had the strength built over years of steady physical exertion; other than straining at times to catch his breath he showed few signs of decline. When he would talk of how all his people had gone, it was sometimes as if they were getting farther and farther away and he feared he might not catch up.

One morning in late June Old Marsh's bed was empty. There was a fast, frantic search around the building, until someone checked the kitchen and saw the back door open. Outside there was a small vegetable garden that a number of staff people tended, and off to the side was a small shed attached to the end of the building, where tools and supplies were stored. Old Marsh, fully dressed, was sitting on the ground leaning against the shed, his feet pushed into the nearest row of seedlings, his old straw hat tipped forward as if to shield his eyes from the slanting, early morning sunshine. And he was dead. Of heart failure, the coroner said. His friends felt it was simply a matter of his soul going off to where his heart had long been, gone from the freshly-dug soil he knew best to be with his people.

The earth was important, too, to Maureen Redl's friend Michael Howell. Redl, who is the founding director of Mill Valley, CA based *Voices of Healing*, began working with Michael on his own healing processes after he was diagnosed with AIDS. The two remained close during the time his illness progressed and after he moved to Amsterdam in order to have medical assistance when he chose to die.

Michael grew up in a well-to-do southern family with all the trappings of success—multiple homes, cars, boats—none of which brought him happiness. After graduating from college he tried working in the family business as had been his father's plan, but found himself as unsuited to that life as he had been to the social fast lane. What Michael loved was living and working with his fellow creatures and the environment that sustains us all. In another life, he said, he would be a veterinarian.

Michael moved to San Francisco and simplified the life he did have, working in several different fields but finding his real satisfaction in volunteer work with environmental groups, primarily those seeking to preserve the endangered wetlands of the San Francisco Bay area. And he came to terms with the fact that his other life was not to be in this timespan, when he was diagnosed HIV-positive.

When he began therapy to deal with the complications of his life and approaching death, Michael sought to use imagery. Wisdom, he found, came to him in the form of an eagle. If there were a special piece of insight to be discovered, his mind would often find it through mental pictures of the powerful creatures he had seen soaring above the rugged Pacific forests or flying free over the ocean.

Growing up, Michael had had no particular spiritual connection. His family worshipped, he sometimes quipped, at the holy Cadillac showroom: "Our holy days were when the new models came out." So he turned, as an adult, to the wisdom of Native American cultures whose ritual and animism struck a responsive chord in his soul. He spoke occasionally of wishing he could simply go off into nature to die as some members of early American tribes had done, becoming once again a part of the food chain and reentering the natural world. When the eagle entered his imaginative thoughts, Maureen felt it a perfect symbol. Because Michael so identified with birds, because he needed the freedom and strength, for a dozen reasons that source of wisdom grew more and more important. And having done its job in life, it was the image of the eagle that Michael chose for his dying—a way of mentally soaring back into the space from which he came.

Early in his illness, Redl says, Michael would often speak of dreams in which he flew on the back of his eagle. But toward the end of his life he said the images began to change. "Eagle is telling me," he reported, "that I'm going to have to fly by myself."

As he grew sicker, and the time when he felt he would ask for help to end his life drew closer, Michael asked Redl to come to Amsterdam for one last visit. He had become wheel-chair-bound, he told her, and was "just one big KS lesion at this point." So she bought plane tickets for early December, 1997. Michael was living on one of the big, floating barges common to the canals of the city, and had two "buddies," Redl says, "as is required in the Netherlands if one is planning an assisted death. It's somewhat like Hospice, only more personal. I had met Walter, one of these young men, on an earlier visit."

Before Redl arrived though, Michael fell, quickly deteriorated, and died within two days. "When I got there, too late, Walter told me about Michael's dying," Redl says. "He and the other friend had not known of Michael's therapy, of course. They said that after he fell they got him into bed, where he started talking non-stop, in a sort of life review. The next day he was quiet, but asked to be propped up in bed, across from a wonderful photo he had taken here on the West Coast of an eagle in flight. Michael wanted the drapes opened.

"His buddies told me he pointed toward the photo without speaking, and then he raised and lowered his arms. Michael flew with his eagle."

I don't know what image Thoreau might have held to when he was dying, but Walden Pond certainly could have sufficed. According to biographer Henry Beetle Hough, Thoreau once wrote, after taking a dip in Walden, that "though the water was thrillingly cold, it was like the thrill of a happy death."

When his time for dying did come, Thoreau was reportedly at peace with the idea. His old Calvinist Aunt Louisa checked in with him about whether he'd made his peace with God, to which Thoreau replied that they'd never quarreled.

The farmer, the woodsman, the naturalist—those whose lives are closely entwined with nature—may have a view of God, heaven, or spiritual reality that leads them, naturally, toward a more open-eyed view of death. "Edward Abbey didn't have to die to find paradise," said novelist Terry Tempest Williams at his memorial service, "he understood and lived it in the here and now."

Those remarks came at a sunrise memorial service in the desert, attended by Abbey's family, friends and fellow writers, shortly after his death in March, 1989. "Only days before (his death)," wrote James Bishop, Jr. in *Epitaph for a Desert Anarchist*, "this disputatious lover of life and nature had finished his 20th book, *A Voice Crying in the Wilderness*, in which he wrote, 'If you feel you're not ready to die, never fear; nature will give you complete and adequate assistance when the time comes'."

Edward Abbey, often criticized for being "an econut" (and worse; he was not shy with his curmudgeonly opinions), discovered the American Southwest when he was a young man and battled his entire life to preserve it as the Eden he first found it to be. To his supporters Abbey was a hero of mythic proportions; to his detractors he was a crackpot, an obstructionist, a radical. But there was never any question about Abbey's ties to the virgin land. His books, essays, speeches are all testaments to his allegiance with the American West.

Of his own mortality, Abbey had written, "To die alone, on a rock under the sun at the brink of the unknown, like a wolf, like a great bird, seems to me to be a very good fortune indeed. To die in the open, under the sky . . . " And according to Bishop's account, Abbey came quite close to fulfilling that prophecy. He was driven by his wife Clarke and several friends to a remote location to watch the stars, though it was back at his writing cabin a few hours later where he actually died.

"One should rehearse one's death from time to time," Abbey had written more than a decade earlier, "so as to perform the part properly when the curtain of eternity does indeed finally rise."

If St. Francis of Assisi did any rehearsing, it had to have been in the way he lived out his days in readiness to meet his God. And his days were among the creatures with whom he gently shared the earth.

"When death was near," writes Lawrence Cunningham in *St. Francis of Assisi*, "he bade them lay him on the bare earth, (saying,) 'I've done what I have had to do; may Christ teach you what you have to do.' He died after sunset; a flight of larks rose in front of the door of the cell."

The symbolism of larks rising—or eagles, in Michael's case, a "great bird" in Edward Abbey's or seabirds in Rachel Carson's—is worth considering. It suggests a release, a freeing, a soaring journey outward. It may be that such associations of living and dying, and associations of dying with other rhythms of nature, come easier to those closely attuned to the earth and its cycles. Or it may just be something their stories invite us to take for ourselves, a song for our own hearing.

Celebrations of Life

If there is one thing guaranteed to evoke differing opinions in discussions of dying it is the issue of celebration. Can one really celebrate life's ending? Or celebrate *at* life's ending? Doesn't that trivialize everything that has come before? I believe the answers are yes, yes and no.

His brother told me Fred's story. Fred died of AIDS at the age of 28, only a few years out of college. He had lived his brief life with such exuberance, by his brother's account, "that you just couldn't help but get caught up in it. I don't think he had an enemy." Fred had accomplished very few of the goals he had in life except one, which was to create beauty. "He used to say creating beauty is what we're put here to do."

Fred had created beauty through classes taught at the florist shop where he worked and through the brightly blooming arrangements that he and his co-workers regularly donated to the nursing home where his grandmother had spent her last years. Mostly, though he created beauty through his friendships. Fred taught friendship, his brother said, the way some people teach piano: learn the basics, pay attention, practice often, and don't be afraid of your mistakes.

When he was dying Fred's friends had what can only be called a celebration. He said he wanted color, and noise, and movement. He didn't feel up to any of it, but that was what he wanted around him. So they brought sunflowers in garish tubs, and hung confetti from the light fixtures, played music as he drifted in and out of consciousness and conducted something akin to an around-the-clock all-American wake. They also cried a lot. But in the process of it all they celebrated, with the dying man, the simple beauty of friendship. It was the kind of friendship that could rejoice with him over the release from what had been truly terrible days and weeks before his death came.

The sculptor James Prestini had been a different kind of friend. A colleague of Mies van der Rohe and part of the Bauhaus architectural movement in Chicago, Prestini joined the faculty of the UC Berkeley School of Architecture in 1956 and was for many years an exacting, hard-driving teacher of design. He had zero tolerance for bad design in anything, whether it was a kitchen appliance or a high-rise building, and little more tolerance for student error.

I met Prestini only after his health had gone into a major decline. He had for years shared a love of garlic, conversation, Italian food and good wine with my husband, and this zest for life, along with his intolerance of slipshod work, were characteristics for which he was widely known. His art survives in the form of bowls made of cherry, birch, mahogany or walnut that are shaped by a lathe into almost unbelievable thinness (a number of which are in the New York Museum of Modern Art, the Metropolitan and other major museums) and cylindrical sculptures of standard steel elements. His reputation survives, in the hearts of friends and former students, for all of the above. I went to his final party, which was as unique as the honoree.

Prestini's friends felt there should be a celebration of his 85th birthday, which seemed clearly destined to be his last. The plan was hampered somewhat by the fact that he was in an intensive care unit at the time. Undeterred, the friends talked a sympathetic nurse into allowing a few decorations and cake and candles (unlit) in the cubicle, and birthday guests to be admitted two at a time for the event.

Because of a traffic jam on the Bay Bridge from San Francisco, my husband and I arrived at the hospital after the declared end-time of the party. The staff sympathy was still holding, however, possibly due to the surreal improbability of it all, and we were ushered to the birthday bedside. Prestini lay surrounded by balloons and ribbons, cards taped to every available surface, a paper crown from the local hamburger place perched jauntily on his head. He seemed to have entered into the celebration. It could have played a part in the remarkable fact that he regained enough strength to leave the hospital and live an additional few weeks in an extended care facility, still surrounded by the friends who celebrated his life.

Prestini's party may have been more for the friends than for the dying man himself, but I don't think that was entirely so.

From the tales that were told, and the celebrations held later at the school of architecture and on a rural hillside where his ashes were placed beneath a sculpture he had created, I think it was consistent with the years before, and whatever follows.

In Mexico, the Day of the Dead is often the liveliest day of the year. A time when the high-spirited living throw a party for and with spirits past, the holiday celebration stands as a meeting point for both sides of the hereafter. It may also provide a useful theory.

What is useful is the suggestion that the celebration of life need not come suddenly to a screeching halt. If that celebration can extend into one's dying—and perhaps even beyond—the life cycle in a sense takes on a new dimension. It is this broadened perspective, rather than any denial of the sadness that also accompanies dying, that argues for celebration as acceptable to the dying process.

Day of the Dead celebrations of course have to do with much more than party time. The day is designated for a reunion between living and dead, a symbolic sharing, once again, of treasures and memorabilia, necessities of life (if not death), favorite foods and good times. The holiday also celebrates the unknown—and what one celebrates one tends not to fear.

Weston Stevens, a Unitarian Universalist minister who has been closely involved with deaths of many kinds, thinks the element of celebration is appropriate. Stevens says he would be in favor of its increase. "We find it perfectly appropriate for a funeral to be a celebration of the life of the deceased," he says; "sometimes death itself begins that celebration."

Stevens thinks his own father's death was such a case. An avid fisherman all his life, the elder Stevens died while pursuing his hobby along a favorite trout stream. "His epitaph was on the dashboard of his car," Stevens says. "It was a note that said, 'Gone Fishin'."

A more deliberate celebration was that staged by renowned artist/printmaker Leo Calapai, a man who lived life to the fullest and was determined to die that way. Calapai was born in Boston of Sicilian immigrant parents just after the turn of the twentieth century. He studied violin as a child, but switched to the visual arts after a move to New York. There he studied mural painting under Ben Shahn, sculpture at the Beaux Arts School of Design and figure drawing at the Art Students League. His long career included one-man shows, the founding of the University of Buffalo's Albright Art School, and completion of a suite of abstract intaglios called "The Seven Last Words of Christ" which is now part of the permanent collection of New York's Metropolitan Museum of Art. Accommodation of his lifelong love of literature led him also into collaborations, as illustrator, with such writers as Thomas Wolfe and William Carlos Williams.

In his ninetieth year, Calapai was given a three-month-long retrospective exhibition by the print department of the Boston Public Library. For the occasion he wrote, at the library's request, a long "narrative statement" cataloguing his achievements and outlining his philosophies of art and life. "I believe," he wrote in the concluding sentence, "that there is no end to one's development and what the future may hold."

Calapai's earthly future was brought short, though, not long after he wrote that line, when he was diagnosed with cancer. It was a rapidly progressing illness, but he announced early in 1993 that he planned to live to celebrate his ninety-first birthday on March 29. "When Leo made the announcement," said his wife Jean some months later, "I took it for granted (that he would do so,) and so did his friends. One, a university professor and friend of many years, made plans to visit—on March 29."

Throughout their thirty-year marriage, Leo Calapai had talked to Jean of how he wished he could have a concert in his own home. When he had first come to New York at the urging of his cousin Vincent Aita, he often joined Aita and a circle of friends who spent Sunday afternoon in each other's homes. There they would listen to performances of chamber music, vocals or instrumental groups, and Leo would be reminded of childhood evenings making music in the living room.

"My parents," Leo said during a talk on his ninetieth birthday, "were very musical, lovers of the operas of Verdi, Donizetti, Bellini and Puccini. They taught me the principal arias, which at the age of eight or ten I sang to their friends, standing on a box in the living room." The same sort of a scene, but with the boy soloist now grown, was what Leo had in mind for his dying.

On March 25, four days before his ninety-first birthday, Leo's physician of many years came to the house to check on the failing health of his patient. He told Leo and Jean that death would likely come in a matter of hours, and that they should finish the signing of papers and documents waiting for completion. Leo asked for the cremation papers, signed several others as Jean and the physician witnessed, and was then helped back into bed. But the desire for the birthday celebration was so strong that Leo and Jean decided they still wanted to put it together. It would be a concert to be held at their home.

Jean reached a pianist friend, Vladimir Leyetchkiss, just as he was leaving to play a concert in Chicago. "I will be with you to play at 7:30, though," Leyetchkiss said. Jean told him the honoree wanted an all-Schubert program.

Jean added new bottles of champagne to three that Leo had recently put in the refrigerator, and together they decided to have crabmeat shipped in from their summer home on an island in Maine's Penobscot Bay. Leo told Jean that when their friend Vladimir had finished the concert she was to play Schubert's "Litany for All Soul's Day" on the piano as she frequently had in the past; "and I said, 'of course'."

Several friends came early on March 29, Leo's birthday, to help make crabmeat canapes. It was while this job was still in progress, after a few of them had been to Leo's room to talk, that his nurse came downstairs with an announcement. "Mr. Calapai," she said, "would like champagne." So the group went upstairs with chilled champagne and glasses, and Leo sat on the side of his bed and toasted his doctors. Then he asked to be lowered back onto his pillows and held up three fingers: it was three hours until concert time.

When Jean went back downstairs to greet the assembled guests she was followed just moments later by the nurse. "Mr. Calapai says you are to play *now*," she said; "he is very urgent." So his wife sat down at the piano and played his favorite pieces until Leyetchkiss arrived. Then began the all-Schubert concert. Leo Calapai slipped into a coma at 8:20, and died an hour and twenty minutes later.

Dying days filled with music and champagne are admittedly unlikely to become commonplace; but celebrations of a sort seem always to have been around. Frontiersman Daniel Boone, according to his biographer John Mack Faragher (in *Daniel Boone*), had a dying event of his own design.

Boone, if one doesn't worry about separating fact from legend, reportedly had a lot to say. "A man needs only three things to be happy: a good gun, a good horse and a good wife." Or more palatably, "If we can't say good we should say no harm;" or "Better mend a fault than find a fault." All of those pearls of wisdom behind him, however, he departed this world with less of a flourish: "I'm going." But he went in fairly festive style.

Having had his portrait done with the help of someone holding his head as he lay dying, Boone called for his coffin and thumped it "to test for soundness." Then he had his hair cut, brushed his teeth (of which he was inordinately proud), and ordered up a song or two from among his favorites. Finally, Boone had everyone file past (family and slaves included) for a kind word of parting.

Dying has changed in the nearly two centuries since. Most of us, especially if we wind up in an institution of one sort or another, will not easily be able to sip champagne and have a friend in to play classical piano. Raucous parties are generally frowned upon in intensive care wards, and forms of dementia will rob many of us of the ability to celebrate our final moments with goodbyes and selected songs.

But dying celebrations may have something to commend them. Certainly a part of the passage for five-year-old Keira Rundlett, whose story is told in chapter 8, was her vision—call it dream, or hallucination, or whatever you choose—of a party complete with birthday cake decorated with pink roses and candles. Others who chose to hasten a death already close at hand did so with candlelight and champagne or with friends singing celebratory songs. Celebrations have something worthwhile to say about the future: what we celebrate, we tend not to fear.

Self-Deliverance

"Once I sat with a friend who was dying of AIDS," Janet said. "We had often said 'I love you,' but this afternoon he seemed to say it more. For a few hours we laughed about good times, and cried about old times . . . and when I left I knew I wouldn't see him again."

She was right. Janet knew, and his doctors knew, and friends knew that others knew, what was openly talked about only within the tight, close circle of his best friends: he had the drugs necessary to end his life. Further, they knew he planned to do so when pain and anguish had overcome all reasons for continuing the struggle. He had detailed information about how to do it comfortably (have a few drinks to relax), quickly (don't stint), and finally (make sure no one calls 911). They called it self-deliverance.

I first heard the term from a kind, indefatigable ex-priest named Richard Wagner, founder of a San Francisco-based organization called Paradigm. Paradigm is a nonsectarian, nonprofit resource center for terminally ill and dying people, who may or may not consider self-deliverance for themselves. "We call our organization Paradigm," Wagner explains, "to signify the need for models of what it can mean to die well in the face of our society's estranged attitudes toward death. Our objective is to familiarize participants with the dying process and engage them in actively improving the quality of their dying."

There is a major distinction between suicide and self-deliverance, Wagner explains. "Suicide is the desperate act of a (physically) healthy person," he says; "self-deliverance is the courageous act of a dying person."

One of the most unusual, and strangely beautiful, self-deliverance stories I've encountered concerns a gutsy 28-year-old woman who lived and died in the 1980s in Wilmington, North Carolina, Gena Jones. Gena worked in the medical records department of Wilmington's New Hanover Regional Medical Center, headed the National Organization of Women chapter in her region, and lived life with energy and passion.

"She was my introduction to feminism," says her close friend Landon Wellford, then an intern at the hospital where Gena worked in the last years of her life. Contrary to his preconceived notions of feminists, "she was one of the nicest, warmest women I ever knew, and, you know, someone who *really* looked good in a dress. She had one or two bad days in her entire life. And as a non-MD, she had more influence than most doctors." Gena lived in a four-room apartment over what had been a carriage house behind one of the city's old homes.

One day, several weeks after having some wisdom teeth pulled, Gena was still experiencing bleeding that medication did not seem to help. When the cause was determined to be cancer, she went to the hospital in Chapel Hill for chemotherapy.

Afterward, "everything was cool," Wellford says. "We had a one-year birthday party when she was N.E.D. (medicalese for No Evidence of Disease) at that point, and you've never seen anybody so grateful. I have pictures of her at that party, standing on the dock, cute, dark-haired, smiling." (Wellford sent some of those pictures to me, to prove that they fairly radiate exuberance.) But two months later the invading cancer was back, and with the particular illness Gena had, "once it recurs, you're basically dead."

The cluster of good friends had by then scattered to other states; Wellford was in Washington, DC. This time Gena went to Duke for additional chemotherapy in an effort to buy time and hope for some new possibilities. When Wellford got there "the ravages of chemo were evident: it hurt her to breathe, it hurt her to talk. She would laugh and then spit up blood." But she wanted to laugh, and Wellford got her to do so by making outlandish sexual suggestions about what they might do if she'd hurry and get out of there. "A steady stream of very significant friends came from all over," he reports, "and her boyfriend, a surgeon, was there. She did get better, got out of isolation, and after five or six weeks of pain that you and I would find intolerable for ten minutes, she got better still. She got her hair back, and got out of the hospital."

Conversations then, though, took a new turn. "She was saying, 'If it gets too bad, can you get me a lethal dose of morphine?' She didn't want to die alone." Wellford and the other young doctors who were close to Gena knew that they could honor her request by pooling supplies of morphine available to them, but it involved a legal issue and moral dilemma that Gena knew was a struggle for them all. Wellford tells of eventually having a mystical experience, which ended with a voice he heard to say "It's not your right." "My friends said, 'Yeah, yeah,' to that," he says. But he had real doubts that he would be able to follow through on any promise to help hasten Gena's death, and knows it would not have been an easy decision for anyone.

Wilmington cardiologist Bill Buchanan, who had not known Gena before her initial illness but had quickly become a good friend, was with her when the fourteen good months came to an end. "She came to me with a rash," he says, "and I knew it had recurred." Buchanan talked with her about a bone marrow transplant, at that time about her only option and one that still held little hope, but Gena chose not to try that procedure.

Out of the hospital and back home, Gena put together a weekend party, with the help of a host of friends and family members who came from scattered distances. It began with a cocktail party on Friday, which Wellford and Buchanan both remember as a time of gaiety and laughter. Buchanan thinks, though, that Gena was already restricting her liquid intake. "She knew if she got dehydrated she would be very, very sick," he says. "She had told us not to rehydrate her, not to do anything."

That Friday, she was very much the old Gena. "You need to understand she was in good spirits, laughing, having a good time," Buchanan says. And Wellford remembers a long conversation the two of them had about his personal life. "It's amazing," he says, "that someone who had no time left still had all the time in the world for you."

On Saturday, Gena shifted the party to a pine grove some distance from town, adjacent to a big house owned by a nonprofit women's organization with which she had long been associated. There, preparations had been made for a "ritual sweat," a purification ritual with ties to several Native American cultures. Gena was entirely comfortable with such rites, Wellford says, having drawn strength from them; others in the group were hesitant. "And the doctors in the group knew it was a form of suicide," he says. "It was clearly, 'I need to die tonight'."

The ritual sweat was anything but a death watch, however. "There was an Indian chieftain there, and we were telling stories of our lives, telling Gena-stories." The gathering centered around a huge pit filled with glowing stones, a sort of giant, outdoor sauna. The liquid that had been in *any* participant's body was little by little removed—throughout a joyous time.

Eventually, "we all stood up and went outside the enclosure," Wellford says. "Gena took about twelve steps, and went down. We took her into the house, showered, and gave her a little morphine; her breathing was getting irregular." Versions of the story differ in small ways, but what everyone agrees was that Gena knew exactly what she was doing, and wanted to do it that way. The doctors, trained to resuscitate, each seemed to have had impulses to strengthen her at one point or another but when one would start to put medical knowledge over Gena's wishes, another would step in.

Like so many others, Gena wanted above everything to die at home. So Wellford arranged a sleeping bag and pillows in the back of his car and started the long drive back down the highway "just praying nobody would try to slow me down." During the somewhat surreal trip, Buchanan turned around to see Gena sit bolt upright and say, in a strong voice from deep in her diaphragm, "I just want to say I love you both. And I'm going to be *ALL RIGHT.*"

Back home Gena, limp but smiling, was met by all of her gathered family and friends. The friends dressed her in white lace, arranged her in her big brass bed, lit candles and put on classical music CDs, and sat with her as she slowly died. "It had the flavor of a country death," Wellford says. "The women washed her and combed her hair, and put her in a different dress. About ten MDs signed that death certificate— and we finally called the funeral home. Then we had a breakfast party, and watched the sun come up."

What Buchanan emphasizes was how Gena's death "brought us all together. She wanted us to realize that death is a part of life, and she wanted not to be remembered in a tragic way." The young cardiologist had already experienced death in the harshest way, when a medical school friend was killed in a boating accident, "something you just don't expect, and especially not *that* person. One of his best friends could not even show up for the funeral."

But Gena, her friends say, taught them another concept of dying. Her brother, with whom she had been particularly close, kept the same spirit throughout her memorial service, making it also a time of laughter and remembrance that was what she had so specifically wanted.

"She knew exactly how to end it, and she did," Buchanan says. "It was a very great gift that she gave the rest of us." Survivors often use that term when their friends have self-delivered, describing themselves as being recipients of a gift.

Daniel, a man old enough to have been Gena's grandfather, faced his own dying a few years later in Seattle, Washington. Daniel was an equally independent soul, and equally passionate about his beliefs. One of those beliefs was that there should be a better way to die than the long, difficult periods he had watched his grandparents go through after each suffered separate strokes.

Daniel lived almost all of his life in New York. He was a self-taught intellectual who read a book a day, mastered several musical instruments and spoke several languages. He made his living free-lancing jobs such as reviewing manuscripts for Columbia Pictures. "He wanted always to be in control of his own life," his daughter Judith explains. "He was brought up Jewish but was an atheist and a socialist."

In the early sixties Daniel suffered a stroke which impaired his ability to play musical instruments or do arithmetic calculations. "He had a series of small strokes over the years," Judith says, "eventually becoming irritable and critical, and having difficulty walking."

Then in 1993, two years before he died, Daniel suffered a massive stroke that left him unable to walk and with difficulty talking and swallowing. "He did physical therapy," Judith says; "the spirit was there, but the damage was irreversible. He became wheelchair bound, and told Mother he was ready to die; but after his doctor prescribed anti-depressants he felt a little better and changed his mind. We learned, though, that with each successive stroke there would be further deterioration of function."

Daniel and his wife moved to Seattle, where his two daughters would be able to help in the extensive care he now required. The family, at Daniel's instigation, came to a tacit understanding about his dying: that when he decided the time had come to end his life no one would argue. "My parents were married for fifty-five years," Judith adds here. "But my mother is a true heroine. She was willing to give him up." The family set about acquiring the barbiturates that would be needed to help him fulfill his last wish.

"For almost a year," Judith says, "we spent a lot of time together. He was a kibitzer, a punster, an arguer. But in what would be the last month of his life he knew his mind was failing and he prized his mind. He began to fear that he would lose the ability to swallow the pills he wanted to swallow."

The day came when Daniel said he wanted to take the pills. So his two daughters and two sons-in-law gathered, along with two of his three grandchildren. "It was very consistent with his life," Judith says. "We knew his value system, we all agreed with him and understood his reasoning; and there was no conflict with our own value systems or beliefs.

"We mixed the barbiturates into a pudding. He was happier than he had seemed in a long time, almost glowing. He knew he looked (that way), and asked me to take his picture a few moments before he lapsed into a coma."

Daniel the jokester also proved himself very much present to his dying. As he dipped the spoon into his pudding, he looked at his assembled family and said, "Wow. Would anybody like to join me for dessert?" Within several hours he was dead.

Robert Lauer faced an equally certain descent into disability when he was diagnosed with Lou Gehrig's disease (ALS) in April, 1989, two months after his first symptoms appeared. An active, self-controlled industrial engineer, Bob Lauer loved camping with his family, playing golf and talking with his friends. He shared with his wife a deep Christian faith.

Lauer's illness progressed with frightening speed. By August, 1989 when he and his wife were taking their son back to school he was wheelchair-bound. Lauer spoke openly with his wife, with the ethics committee of his hospital, and his minister about his illness and his options. He understood that the progression of the disease would necessitate eventually a stomach tube, then a respirator; he declined.

"One of the things about this disease," explains Deanna Lauer, "is that the brain is not affected. Bob was able to make very clear what he wanted, even though at the end he could only move his little finger and blink his eyes. He also required a breathing mask (the last step before the respirator) and was able to be out of the mask for only three minutes at a time."

After making his wishes known and assuring himself that his family understood, Bob Lauer entered the hospital.

His doctor gave him a shot of morphine and removed the mask, but at the end of three minutes it was not replaced.

"Quality of life for Bob," says Deanna Lauer, "was being able to communicate, being able to move. I think he took into consideration his own feelings, the fact that he didn't want to live as a vegetable. But I think he was also being considerate of the family and what we were going through with him. I'm glad his dying happened the way it did. I would never have wanted to make that decision."

Over and over, in discussions about living wills and right-to-die legislation and the agonizing decisions facing dying people and their loved ones today, the question of self-deliverance is raised.

For some it is morally or ethically wrong or against their religious beliefs and out of the question. For others, and I am in this group, it is a choice we think we might make but have no idea if we could actually do so. For Gena Jones, Daniel, Bob Lauer, and hundreds of others, self-deliverance has been a testimony to their determination to die unafraid.

Mystery and Meaning

Skepticism has always appealed to me more than mysticism. I find it fascinating when friends turn up ghosts in their attics or discover previous incarnations or truly believe in manifestations of the spirit world—but a part of me always wants to say, "Yes, then how do you explain *this*?" In the real world, the pragmatic self argues, one can find rational explanations if one takes time to look.

I have given up that attitude where dying is concerned.

If dying could be fully understood and explained, in fact, living itself would be diminished. For some of us at least, living without the anticipation of something larger, deeper and potentially more meaningful ahead, something beyond human comprehension, would make living either too empty or too much a burden. We come to see dying, therefore, as a doorway to that mysterious Otherness. And when we encounter those whose dying has mystic overtones their stories are somehow reassuring.

My first such encounter was on an icy February day in 1987. At my father's request I had booked a flight from Florida to Richmond, Virginia to visit his nearby home in Ashland. It had been a complicated arrangement, because he had specified the previous Thanksgiving that he wanted my sister Jane and me to be there together. Ever since my mother's death 20 years earlier we children and (later) grandchildren had made independent trips to Ashland whenever possible, because my father got so much mileage out of each visit. He reveled in advance plans and discussions with anyone who would listen, in alerting the local newspaper and issuing invitations for lunch and dinner parties at the local Holiday Inn dining room, then Ashland's finest.

This time was different. He repeatedly stipulated that the two of us were to come together. He gave no reason. But of his four daughters Jane, the eldest, who lived in Alabama, was the executor of his estate and I, the youngest, was the writer and designated family scribe. It took several months to work out schedules and details, but Jane and I eventually met in Atlanta to catch a connecting flight to Richmond. When we got to the Atlanta airport we learned that Richmond was snowed in and its airport closed. We called my father and reported that we hoped to get in the next day; he was his usual cheerful self.

I used the time in Atlanta for a telephone visit with my former mother-in-law, Laurette Fossett, with whom I had remained close although her son and I had divorced. She was also in high spirits as we talked about her grandchildren and the events of the day.

Jane and I caught what would be the first flight to land in Richmond when the airport reopened the next morning. We picked up a rental car and carefully negotiated US 95 North and the much chancier streets of Ashland. Most of the town was closed up tight by the snowstorm but Dad was determined to stick with his lunching-out plan so we inched our way to a local saloon serving soup and crackers to the very brave or very hungry. Afterward, he was impatient to get back home.

We sat in the familiar living room of my father's house, Jane and I, listening to his traditional monologue. It consisted of a survey of his twelve absolutely flawless grandchildren, grouped by family, encapsulating the past and present achievements of each and summarily dismissing any imperfection which might have insinuated itself into their lives.

"Oh, she did have a problem with such-and-such," he would say, "but you know, she's got that firmly under control now. She's just fine now, by Jove, just fine." It was not necessary to respond to these monologues, a regular feature of every visit with my father; one had only to nod from time to time while he satisfied himself as to the remarkable goodness of his posterity.

My father then began a brief report on his own physical status. An intensely private man, he was never able to articulate personal issues. He did on this day, however, mention that he had experienced, from time to time, "a little heat around my heart. Nothing to worry about, you understand, just a little heat, around here." He patted his chest. We suggested that perhaps he might consider a trip to the Birmingham hospital where Jane's husband was a teaching physician and where Dad had been years before for cancer surgery. Hospitalization in nearby Richmond, where attention would be drawn to his physical condition, was simply unthinkable. We suggested, though, that a check-up might be in order.

"Yes, I see," said my father. "Well, I'll think about it." Then he shuffled briskly down the hall to his room and closed the door.

When we called him to dinner several hours later there was no answer. We found my father in a kneeling position on the floor, at the head of his bed, where he had said his prayers for nearly ninety years.

Earl Moreland was a praying man, an ebullient optimist with an enormous amount of self-confidence who nevertheless believed in daily consultation with his maker. It had been ever thus: when he went from his native Texas as an educational Methodist missionary to Brazil in the early 1920s, when he took over the presidency of then virtually broke Randolph-Macon College in 1939 and negotiated it through the stormy, tiny-enrollment days (the college was all-male at the time) of World War II, or while he read Keats and Homer and the daily newspapers to my mother throughout the invalid years before her death. Invariably his actions were taken in the supreme confidence that this was a matter discussed and settled upon by himself and God. Looking at him just dead, I couldn't help but believe that he and God were having a little talk about whether this mightn't be a good time to die. How *long* they had been discussing the issue—since Thanksgiving at least, it seemed—is also interesting to consider in hindsight.

Laurette Fossett was somewhat less an optimist, but Earl's equal in the daily prayer department, in determination and sheer gumption. Born simultaneously with the new twentieth century, she grew up motherless in Chicago, the youngest of thirteen children, and raised two of her own through the Depression years while married to a charismatic, risk-taking real estate speculator. She and Earl, though living in different states, became friends quickly when their children married. They stayed in touch after the deaths of their spouses and after the fairly amicable divorce of their children.

Among the causes Laurette espoused was creation of her county's first public nursing home for elderly and incapacitated citizens with nowhere else to go. From its beginning in the mid-1950s until almost the time of her own death she worked to make the final days of Mountain View Rest Home residents as meaningful as possible.

But her own experience with others' dying lay behind one of Laurette's most passionate assertions: she intended to die in her own living room, seated in her own easy chair with her feet on the footstool, coffee mug at one hand and TV remote at the other. For years she had repeated this plan to all who would listen.

When I called my daughter in Georgia to tell her of her grandfather's death, late on that February afternoon, she said she thought she'd go over to Laurette's apartment rather than give her such news over the phone. In the apartment Laurette was found seated in her own easy chair, coffee mug at one hand and TV remote at the other. Also nearby were some documents relating to her will, the only indication that she had had some premonition of an approaching death.

Had they deliberately reached out to participate in their dying processes, these two independent souls who shared an unshakable conviction that they were going to some better place? We'll certainly never know on this side of the hereafter. Their death certificates list times barely ten minutes apart. And their grandson observed that his grandfather "went ahead, to get there first and hold the gate."

Something equally unexplainable happened in the dying days of a hospice patient of Jacquelyn Kanya-Matzen's in Palo Alto, California. Olga (a fictitious name, as is that of her sister) had been a 13-year-old in her native Germany when World War II began raging around her, and she had been forced to leave home and go to work to survive. Her sister Helen, five years younger, stayed home in what Olga always believed were kinder circumstances. Bitter and resentful, Olga eventually lost contact with her sister, married, moved to the United States, and raised two children here.

Younger sister Helen suffered, in fact, far more than Olga, living from hand to mouth for much of her childhood and seeing her mother raped by Russian soldiers when she was barely ten years old. She knew of Olga's marriage, but harbored her own bitterness and made no attempt to maintain contact when her sister moved across the Atlantic.

One day, for reasons she never understood, Helen felt an urge to try to contact the sister she had last seen nearly half a century earlier. Remembering her brother-in-law's name and the general area to which they had moved, she picked up the phone and began searching for such a family in the San Francisco Bay area. Eventually she reached her sister's home and a 19-year-old niece who was not even aware of Helen's existence.

"My mom," said the niece, "is very sick and in the hospital here." Olga was, in fact, expected to die at any moment. Helen got on an airplane and flew to California. When the two sisters met, Olga's physical condition was beyond improving, but her emotional state took a huge turn for the better and she was able to go home to die. "I feel more peace now," she told Jackie. Reunited with family members *she* never knew existed, Helen returned to Germany. But what powerful spirit moved between the younger woman and her dying sister, to bring it all about, no one knew.

I believe such spirits exist, whether we understand them to be the presence of God or the power of the universe, an earlier incarnation or cosmic vibrations; for all we know about communications there is infinitely more that remains unknown.

It is this very unknown-ness that sometimes seems to transcend reality and make fearless dying happen. Paradigm director Richard Wagner tells a fascinating story of visiting a young man who was dying of AIDS in a San Francisco hospital room. One day the young man seemed unusally bright and cheerful, and told Wagner the reason. He had had a dream, he said, about all the men who had died similarly in that room. "And when I woke up," he explained, "they were all here, standing around laughing and talking, as if this were a sort of a party. We had the best time."

Wagner didn't contradict his friend's perception. "What do we know," he says in reflection: "dreams, hallucinations, spirits? All we really know is that we don't know."

Which has, for me at least, a comforting sort of ring to it.

There is further comfort in the realization that some who have died before us seem to have quietly made contact with that mysterious connectedness, and it seems not frightening in the least. Deanna Lauer believes that to have been the case with her husband, whose story is told in the previous chapter.

The Lauers had sold their Pennsylvania home and bought a place in North Carolina to which they planned to retire. But when Robert Lauer became ill the couple decided to stay in Pittsburgh and rent out the North Carolina house. After her husband's death, Deanna struggled with the decision about what should be done with the place that had represented such now-vanished future happiness. Eventually she opted to sell, and travelled south to make arrangements for putting it on the market.

It was during this trip that "I was standing in the kitchen, and I turned to the left, and Bob was standing there with a grin on his face. I saw it as him telling me it was OK, to go ahead and get rid of it," Deanna says quite matter-of-factly. There is no question in her mind but that her husband was briefly, but absolutely, present.

Similar stories have been widely documented over the years, and for every story there is a theoretical explanation. My preference is for Richard Wagner's comment: "What do we know? All we really know is that we don't know."

Among the illnesses we don't know, Alzheimer's is one of the most baffling, and certainly among the most heart-breaking for families and friends. Jean McKenzie Oast watched with the rest of her family as her father, a respected Alabama businessman, slipped into the darkness of Alzheimer's. But an experience that took place as he was dying left Jean with a curious sense of peace, of something within her dying father that was stronger than the disease.

Richardson McKenzie and his wife had often talked together in the darkness of their bedroom. Long after he had withdrawn from reality, and essentially ceased to communicate with his loved ones, McKenzie could be heard talking again. Jean caught his voice sometimes late at night, on a visit from her own home in the days before his death. One night, consumed with curiosity, she crept quietly into his room and sat on the floor at the end of his bed.

What she heard was not the voice of illness. Turned away from the side of his twin bed which had faced his wife, her father was speaking in a firm, almost youthful voice into the darkness. "There was a man, Richardson McKenzie," he was saying; "he always tried to be a *good* man . . ." It was a one-way conversation, but Jean believes her father was not just talking into the air. Her father, she feels certain, "was arguing his case with God."

When McKenzie died, his family found details of the case he had been pleading which they had not known. Answering the phone a few days later, Jean spoke with an elderly black woman she had never met. The woman said she and her family had for years had a difficult time, but they were helped through it all by monthly checks sent by McKenzie, on the condition that no one would be told. "In this house," the stranger said, "we call his name blessed."

We may not all have our names called blessed, or make contact with loved ones from this side of the grave or the other, or manage to die precisely as we'd hoped. We do, though, all share the certainty that our lives will come to an end. And the things we *don't* know about the time thereafter may just have a relationship to the time before. Such a possibility at least—whether one sees it in the context of a right-eous life promising eternal peace or a proper existence in this mortality guaranteeing better luck in the next incarnation—makes the mysteries themselves of interest.

One of the strangest of mysteries is the premonition. Two well-known figures on the world stage are among those reported to have had premonitions of their early deaths, United Nations Secretary General Dag Hammerskjold in this century and Wild Bill Hickok in the 19th. Each had some sound basis for apprehension—Hammerskjold dealing with the incendiary conditions of a fragmented world as he struggled to help build the fledgling UN into a force for peace and Hickok living as he did in a time (1837-1876) and place (the appropriately called Wild West) when lives were lived hard and fast. But it is interesting to look at these examples of one more mystery of life.

Dag Hammarskjold, a renowned Swedish statesman, was elected Secretary-General of the United Nations in 1953 and subsequently named to a second consecutive term. His tenure was marked by repeated journeys to China, Africa and the Middle East in attempts to lessen tensions and advance the cause of peace. Hammarskjold was active in developments taking place in the Republic of Congo (now Zaire) against fierce opposition from the Soviet Union, and it was on one such mission to Congo that his plane crashed in Northern Rhodesia (now Zambia,) killing those aboard.

Some of Hammarskjold's closest friends think he had some sense of impending death when he left on that final journey. They cite two uncanny facts: his leaving the draft of the introduction to his final U.N. Report with the comment,

"I don't see what I can write after this one" and what he took along on that fateful trip, one book only. It was *The Life of Christ.* Tucked within its pages was a copy of the oath of office for U.N. Secretary General. Hammarskjold received a posthumous Nobel Peace Prize.

Sudden death certainly came more predictably and more frequently in Hickok's day, particularly if one embraced the rather hazardous career he chose. In his brief lifetime Hickok served as a frontier marshal, Civil War scout, gunfighter, showman and stage driver. It was during his days as a marshal in Fort Riley, Hays and Abilene, Kansas that he gained fame as a marksman in encounters with outlaws. Hickok's last such enounter was the one in which he lost out to his killer, Jack McCall in Deadwood (now South Dakota).

Biographer Joseph G. Rosa tells, in *They Called Him Wild Bill,* of the words Hickok wrote to his bride of two weeks shortly before his final gunfight: "Agnes Darling, If such should be we never meet again, while firing my last shot I will gently breathe the name of my wife—Agnes—and with wishes even for my enemies I will take the plunge and try to swim to the other shore." The week before he did indeed fire that last shot, according to newspaper reports of the time, he also remarked to a friend that his "days were numbered; my sun is sinking fast . . ."

Soldiers going off to battle, of course, regularly pen such notes to loved ones they may never see again, and presumably both good guys and bad guys employed in the gunslingers' trade of the Wild West often felt their days were numbered. But sometimes, I think when those numbers are about to be called there are signals that only those involved can read.

Anne Sumers spent the night with her brother Rick (whose story is told in chapter 12) one or two days before he died. "This was so odd," she says. "Late in the evening he woke up and asked, 'What do the writings say?' I said, 'This message is only for you.' But it was a message of joy."

Did Earl Moreland read such messages or feel such signals and choose to wrap up his life in an extraordinary final few hours? Did Bob Lauer in fact communicate with the wife who had stood by his final struggles? Did Dag Hammarskjold feel the imminence of his death and manage a summation of things most significant to his life? The questions seem less important to me than the reassurances offered in the stories, whether the stories are *true* or not.

And it *is* true: all we know is that we don't know.

Big Gifts from Small Sources

When I was very young, I remember visualizing dying as a sort of romance, an exotic mystery that held a great deal of fascination but no particular threat. Probably because no one essential to me had died and was therefore gone forever, or because my references were books like *Snow White*, death and dying suggested glamour of a transient sort rather than loss of a wrenching, permanent sort. When I was about seven the mother of one of my neighborhood best friends died in a winter storm accident, the first such tragedy to touch my life in a peripheral way. But rather than any real sadness for my friend (who seems not to have resented that callousness over all these years), what I remember feeling most was envy over all the attention she was getting—plus a consuming curiosity about what her mother's dying had been like. And I remember, before and after those months, poring over books with pictures of the temporarily-dead Snow White or the mystically-dead small children in Russian folk tales. The dead children were always beautiful.

As I would learn decades later, neither my morbid childhood curiosity nor my romanticized fascination were particularly unusual. I was wandering through, I suppose, the childish stages of understanding one's own mortality. Psychologist Maria H. Nagy, writing on *The Child's View of Death* (reprinted in Herman Feifel's *The Meaning of Death*, McGraw-Hill, 1959), explains that children under five usually don't recognize death as irreversible fact. Bad things happen but then they're over; mommy leaves, but she comes back later. Between the ages of (approximately) five and nine, Nagy says, children tend to personify death, to see it as "a contingency." It is only later that dying is seen as a process "which happens to us according to certain laws." All along, say Nagy and others, we are curious.

Whatever the coping mechanisms young children come equipped with, they are often able to face their own dying with much more ease and grace than their grieving parents. In the end the child may become the comforter. Having never lost a child, I can only imagine the unbearable sadness and pain such an experience would bring. But in encountering stories of children coming to terms with their own dying I got a glimpse into how the parent may survive—and how the child may draw on a strength that can't quite be explained.

A case in point was the short, prescient life of an Indiana child named Andrew Warrer. Riding in a car with his mother one summer day when he was four, Andrew remarked, "You know, Mommy, I'm not going to live to be six years old. But you don't have to worry about it. Everything's going to be okay."

His mother put the comment aside as the likely result of some recent story or combination of fables and dreams. When he had repeated it to her, and later to his father, though, they became concerned. At Christmastime, when he was diagnosed with a rare, lethal form of cancer, their concern turned to terror.

Over the months that followed, Andrew's parents traveled the continent in a vain, frantic search for a cure. They kept their son at home with them against the advice of his doctors, who worried both about their patient and about his parents having to cope with the increasingly gruesome nature of his illness. Andrew's cancer began with a tumor on his pelvis which eventually grew outside of his body.

Andrew's father Bruce Warrer, a retired police officer, speaks of those months as a nightmarish rollercoaster veering between joy and despair. Because the family lived some distance from town and no playmates his own age were nearby, Andrew had spent almost all of his brief life among adults. His father suspects that this circumstance led to the traits of language and behavior that made Andrew seem wise beyond his years. It also led to the family's being extraordinarily close-knit.

Shortly before Andrew's death, he and his father were lying together on his bed when the tiny youngster suddenly stirred, opened his eyes wide and said in a bright, clear voice, "You know, Poppy, I don't live here any more." Andrew died at the end of his fifth year. He was buried two days before his sixth birthday.

What his father remembers, as much as (and gradually more than) the pain of those long months of illness, is the equanimity with which Andrew faced his imminent death. Though heavily sedated once his cancer spread, he seemed to have known long in advance of his parents that his stay on earth would be brief, and to view this as perfectly all right. "His philosophy seemed to be," his father says, "that he'd had lots of lives and would have lots more—this one was brief, but had been pretty good for the most part."

They did not address the subject of dying specifically, Bruce Warrer says. "But it was as if he constantly wanted to reassure us that everything would be all right, and we should not worry."

This ability of very young children to see life as forever and death as temporary is peculiarly close to the ways in which many adults manage to die unafraid. Grown-ups turn to a belief in the hereafter, in reincarnation, or a concept of a broader cosmos which extends beyond mortal life; children may come equipped with the ability to form similar, but simpler views: Other bad things have come and gone; dying is just one more bad thing that will pass.

Bruce Warrer says, reflecting on the life and death of his son, that Andrew seemed to have such a viewpoint, a way of mixing reality with fantasy and dreams to fashion an acceptable way of living his own dying, unafraid.

Keira Rundlett was another child with a remarkable ability to fashion an acceptable framework for her own dying. Keira suffered from the time she was just a few months old with heart and lung problems that eventually caused her death in 1980, at the age of five years and six months. For much of her brief life, though she was quite fragile and unable to share the rambunctious activities of other children, she was relatively pain-free. But like Andrew Warrer, she seemed to develop her own sense of dying and her own ways of coming to terms with it all.

"There were comments that struck us as so strange," recalls her mother, Melissa Skelton. "She would say something like, 'I'm going away, and you won't be seeing me any more . . . ;' and this would be brightly announced, in contrast with her (extreme) fear of being left alone."

Keira's father, Brad Rundlett, then studying to become an Episcopal priest, says he and his daughter "did not ever talk about death per se. She would ask questions about why God made her that way . . . and I never had an answer." The Rundletts, like grieving parents before and since, tried every route possible in a desperate search for help; but several months before her fifth birthday Keira began a rapid decline.

"She became cyanotic, her skin ashen, and began to have seizures which seemed very painful and would last as long as twenty or thirty seconds," her father says. "Two days before her death she had an extremely bad seizure. All of us were with her, and she said, 'I'm going to leave you.' She was purple, and looked to be in terrible pain, but her voice was calm, and very clear. I remember being amazed at the tone of her voice."

But Keira did recover, and Brad Rundlett says they then talked about what had happened.

"She told me she had seen something, and I said, 'What did you see?' She said, 'Lots of people standing around a cake, a cake with white icing and with pink roses all around it. They were waiting.'

"I said, 'Were they waiting for you?' and she smiled and said, 'No,' as if I were being silly. 'They were waiting to eat the cake'."

Keira's family thought, then, of how they had not celebrated her last birthday because she had been sick with pneumonia. So her father left, after Keira assured him she was fine, to go shopping for birthday presents. While he was gone Keira had a final seizure.

"It was almost like she was in a twilight consciousness," her mother says. "And then she said, 'I feel like I'm flying'."

Often people who have lost someone very close to them tell of having dreams about being with the now-dead person which are so vivid that on waking the smell or touch is still present. Brad Rundlett remembers several such dreams. He also recalls a dream tied to Keira's last words.

"A very nice, elderly man I'd never seen before, about five feet four or five inches tall, Caucasian, kind of paunchy and balding, was holding her hand, and they just took off flying," Rundlett recalls. "My sense was that he was showing her the world."

The world of the dying child expands and contracts in ways beyond his control, often in ways that produce courage and wisdom beyond his years. That was the case with Philip, a 10-year-old California boy whose parents had divorced when he was just starting school, and whose story was told by his hospice worker Jacquelyn Kanya-Matzen. His mother moved out of the state after the divorce, leaving Philip in the care of his immigrant father. Philip was already suffering from the leukemia that had been diagnosed when he was a preschooler.

Philip's father, who ran a small trade shop, turned for help to a woman nearby who was raising a son, David, a year younger than Philip. The two boys became friends, but it was a tenuous friendship, strained by the constant attention that Philip required from David's mother for medications and trips to the doctor or hospital. By the time Philip's condition had worsened to the point where hospitalization was required, David was refusing even to go and visit his friend.

Kanya-Matzen, recognizing a severe case of jealousy aggravated by fear of the whole hospital scene, prevailed upon David to conquer those feelings just enough to pay a farewell visit. She reports a moving encounter between the two:

"While I'm losing my life," Philip said, "I want you to know I'm thankful to you for sharing your mom."

David swallowed hard. "Well, I'm not jealous any more," he said. "Because I'm glad I don't have to go through all those tubes and stuff."

"Maybe," said Philip, who knew the approximate location of his long-absent parent, "I'll go visit my mom." The comment was straightforward and matter-of-fact, as if, for Philip, dying were simply a way of making the connection he wished for, but had been denied, in living.

Long before any of the above stories took place, another child dealt with her own dying and her own family relationships in a manner suggestive of a bygone era, yet still consistent with the world of the pre-teenager. In the summer of 1928, 11-year-old Ruth Lovejoy finished her last day of school in tiny Union, South Carolina and went home complaining

that she felt bad. By the time her stomachache had been identified as appendicitis and young Ruth had been taken to the
hospital in an adjoining community, little could have saved her
life except the miracle drugs that were then undiscovered.

So Ruth, alone in a hospital room on what she seemed
to recognize as the night she was dying, set about putting her
affairs in order. On small, pink note cards that her grandmother had brought she wrote notes to her sisters reassuring
them about her care ("I just had some grape juice and two ani-
mal crackers . . . ") and bearing long lines of X's and O's.

When she came to the final note her handwriting was
barely legible, but in an 11-year-old sense Ruth seemed equal
to the self-assigned task:

"Dear Mother and Dad," she wrote. "I have been mean
and I am so sorry. Please forgive me so much. Love, Ruth.
P.S., I can't write good. Please don't cry. I must say goodbye."

Ruth Lovejoy, whose sisters still treasure the small, pink
notes, died at a time when friends and family usually
attended the dying and entire communities rallied around
survivors. (It was also an age when children were admon-
ished never to be mean, but to be "good little boys and girls.")
The local papers were full of articles clipped and saved by her
family that could only have been written in that flowering
period of small-town journalism. The stories attest to her
"lovable disposition and appealing personality . . .," and
boldly assert that as a "patient sufferer, she (wished) only to
go home or to heaven." But whatever her traits and wherever
she went, it is interesting to note the parallels between stories like Ruth's and stories of children like Philip nearly
three-quarters of a century later.

The last time I saw my cousin Martha's young daughter she was still months away from her own death, but I think she may have been handling that reality better than anyone suspected—and better than was possible for her grieving family. Years later I listened to the tapes she had made about her life. I was struck by her anger at the cancer that had robbed her first of her ability to walk and eventually of all other physical strength, but I was even more impressed with how calmly she spoke of her life in the past. Although her family was doing everything possible to enhance and preserve her life, Jean often sounded almost impatient to put it behind her—as if this was enough of this, and she were ready to get on to something else, something hopefully better.

Most of everything, Jean Canter had treasured her mobility. She loved walking the Alexandria, Virginia neighborhood where she delivered newspapers to then-vice-president Gerald Ford. She loved walking around the nation's capitol, or walking the beaches where her family vacationed every summer. So when she began to fall, and later had to take to a wheelchair, one of the hardest facts of life was that she could no longer tie up her shoelaces and take off walking.

Jean fought hard against the disease, and against the gradual loss of independence. She stubbornly pursued the goals she could, including propelling herself across the stage to accept a hard-won high school diploma. But hers was a relentless cancer that eventually left her immobilized and totally dependent on her family's care. She had two last wishes. One, which she and her mother quietly attended to one afternoon, was to choose the spot where she would be buried. It provided a bridging between life and death, the selection of a shady patch of hillside. The second wish was in a sense a gesture forward, toward an afterlife she had come to believe was also a good space, and a gesture backward toward the days before her steps became too heavy to walk in the sand: when Jean Canter died, and was buried in the spot she had chosen, her once-lively feet were carefully shod in a brand new pair of saddle oxfords.

I don't know whether stories like these, all told by people who loved these children and had to find ways to keep on living when they were gone, truly represent instances of children and young people dying unafraid. But I think they do. It is another case of our knowing only that we don't know . . . and we don't know the sources of strength and peace that children seem sometimes able to tap, at a time when they need them most.

Beholding Beauty

Images of dying are images of ugliness. Those images, the pictures that most of us carry around in our heads, come from seeing the victims of violence on TV or the devastation that sickness—and sometimes its treatments—wreaks upon those we know and love. The physical face of dying, unless one happens to be a movie heroine in her final moments, is seldom a pretty face.

And there is no escaping the equation: Youth + Health = Beauty. It's a part of our cultural image, a part that gets reinforced all day long from every possible angle—media, advertising, career paths, casual conversation among friends and relatives. Further, the youth/health/beauty syndrome has come to be synonymous with what is desirable, or even in many cases what is minimally acceptable.

So what is one to do with dying, which hardly meets these desirability requirements? Especially if the dying happens to be one's own?

The first time my own acceptance of the youth + health = beauty equation was dramatically challenged was through a hospice patient I will call Bernard. He was middle-aged (although you'd have thought him eighty-five at least) and dying, but so secure in the understanding of his own beauty that I began to understand it myself. Bernard, who was actually probably no handsome hunk when he was young and healthy, was so smilingly at home in the presence of the afflictions visited upon him as he lay dying that it became impossible not to see him as, well, *gorgeous.*

Bernard gave me, in fact, two huge gifts: the ability to see beauty and the secret to fearlessness. He was fearless about his unlovely dying.

An alcoholic of long standing, Bernard was dying of a combination of cirrhosis of the liver, metastasized cancer and an assortment of other physical problems. None of them were pretty. He was gaunt and sulphur-colored, missing most of his teeth and thoroughly hairless; his toenails and fingernails had thickened into unmanageable shells and his long limbs seemed hooked to their fragile frame by loose wires. He had lesions scattered around his body that were (he said) "harder on the looker than on yours truly."

Bernard's long-suffering wife Marie had multiple sclerosis. She could get around with the help of a walker, but was unable to do anything more than the simplest of household tasks. The two of them depended on a visiting nurse for minimal care, and irregular help from friends and neighbors (they had no family anywhere nearby) for the rest. When I paid my first call as their newly-assigned volunteer I suggested that maybe what they needed most and I could do best was mop the floor.

Our relationship progessed, over a matter of months, pretty much along these lines: I would drop by and do some cleaning or laundry, bring groceries or supplies from the store, and listen to Bernard tell stories. He was usually the hero of his stories. I marvelled at the fact that Marie could still smile at them, and particularly at how they were told not with a sense of long-lamented-past but with the sense of a life that was still being lived with gusto. He had conquered his alcoholism in time to enjoy some sane and sober years, but his stories swept from chaos to sobriety with abandon.

As an unskilled volunteer without medical training, I was not involved in Bernard's care. I did, though, a lot of face-washing and nail-filing (a podiatrist friend gave me an implement more like a saw than a file) and hand-holding when Marie was gone on errands. And the closer I got, the more I saw Bernard as actually handsome. One day when I was putting away some laundry I stopped and stared at the picture on Marie's dresser which showed the two of them shortly after their marriage. Bernard, with one long arm around plump, beaming Marie, had a mass of wavy black hair and was grinning at the camera with a devil-may-care self confidence. I realized that the man in the picture was not that far from the man I had come to see behind the yellowed skull on the pillow—even though I'd never known him with the healthy tan and lush hairdo. It was almost as if Bernard with his raspy voice and failing body, had been willing me to see through to the whole man.

One afternoon when I was working in my garden a frantic call came from Marie. Bernard had lost bowel and bladder control, she said, her voice breaking. He was in misery. It happened to be the day of the Hospice picnic, which I'd been unable to attend but to which, it seemed, every healthcare professional in the county had gone.

"I'm grimy dirty myself," I said, "but let me just throw on a clean shirt and wash my hands and I'll be right over." I did that as quickly as I could, hopped in my car and was halfway to their house—not more than ten minutes' drive—when I realized what was happening.

"What *AM* I doing?!" I asked myself. "Here I am, still new to all this. I can't *possibly* deal with cleaning up a shriveled, yellowish, dying man." But I reckoned myself too grown-up—or too embarrassed—to turn around. So with a mounting sense of hopeless incompetence and impending doom, I kept driving.

Marie pulled her walker up to one side of the hospital bed where Bernard lay. I got on the other side, managed to haul the dead weight of Bernard's long legs over my shoulder and wrestled the soiled clothes and linens from beneath him with Marie's help. Eventually, using the same procedure, we got him cleaned up and into fresh clothes, on fresh, clean sheets. But midway through, Marie and I got the giggles. Bernard was only barely conscious and fortunately did not seem in pain; it would not have mattered. The contortions we were going through to see this project completed were such that we either had to laugh or cry.

After we were through, and I had started the washing machine and put away the basket of cleaning tools, I mopped my face and said I'd better get back to the garden. But I went first into Bernard's room, where he now seemed thankfully asleep, to kiss his forehead before I left. As I did so, he reached up for a hug.

"If you thought you were feeling bad before I got here," I said, "you must be feeling absolutely awful now. I apologize for all that slinging around."

"S'okay," he whispered. Then he winked one sunken eye and flashed a brief smile. I can't imagine where he got the strength.

As I skipped down the three steps from Bernard's front porch, I remember feeling a sense of power I had never known. If I could do *that*, I told myself, well, *nothing* was impossible. That has not proved exactly true, but in the years since Bernard died I have said a hundred prayers of thankfulness for him.

At about the same time of Bernard's dying days in Florida, Hospice worker Jacquelyn Kanya-Matzen had a longshoreman patient in northern California. He was also jaundiced and wasted, suffering from rotting teeth and nicotine withdrawal, and dying of cancer that had spread from his lungs to his liver.

"He told me he had pacts with God and the devil both," Kanya-Matzen says. "He said, 'I've been in heaven and I've been in hell, and decided it doesn't make much difference where I wind up now.' But in spite of everything he'd been through and the shape he was in by the time I got to know him, his spirit was so strong that I always thought him handsome."

Kanya-Matzen never knew her longshoreman friend in his healthy days. She had no images of him other than those generated by his physical presence—and his spiritual strength. But that latter, she recalls, made an indelible impression of vitality and beauty that overrode any contemporary truth. She knows there was ugliness; she remembers him for his beauty.

Meg was someone who had in fact been known for her beauty. Before she met her husband Dave she had worked for a New York modeling agency, appearing in newspaper and magazine ads, corporate brochures and such. She said she'd never even come close to "the big time," but she continued to work in modeling off and on for several decades. She was in her mid-forties when she was diagnosed with cancer.

Dave had a picture of Meg that she'd given him when they first met, a portrait shot from her early publicity photos. In it, she was resting her chin on the back of her hand, nonchalantly holding a pencil in two fingers. She told him she thought they'd come up with that to show she photographed well as a glamorous secretary or businesswoman. It was the expression that he loved, though, half-pensive, half-coquette. After she got sick, Dave used to tell her he could squeeze her hand and see the girl with the pencil.

Ferociously fighting for more time on earth, Meg was ravaged by both her illness and the medical efforts to keep it at bay. But as it became clear that none of those efforts would succeed she faced her dying with extraordinary grace. "I know what I look like," she said a few days before she died, "and I know what death looks like. Neither of us are very pretty any more on the outside. But inside, we're friends."

Dave said that death was no friend of his, and he didn't have any interest in knowing what it looked like. "But you should," she replied. "It's OK. Especially after all I've come through to see it." Then she smiled just the slightest bit and said, "Squeeze my hand, Dave. Squeeze both hands."

"So I did," he said later. "I didn't see what death looked like, or even, that time, the girl with the pencil. But I felt this huge sense of peace, like it really *was* OK."

My friend Bob Bowron would, in all likelihood, find it laughable to be remembered for his beauty. He often looked as if he'd just been too busy to bother with combing his hair or worrying about what to put on, and that was equally often the case.

A boistrous man with a wide grin usually stretched across his craggy face, Bob was never shy with his opinions. He also had some notoriety for the outlandish. Once, when called upon to make an announcement about an up-coming conference at the fairly sedate church he and I both attended, he arose from a rear pew, strode down the aisle booming out a verse from "Goodnight Irene" that he felt applied to his message and said his piece. When the news came that he was dying of a fast-spreading cancer I wrote him that he would hang around in my life for a long time. Whenever I felt in need of a little gumption, I told him, I would simply call on my inner Bob Bowron. And in the years since his death I have done that more than once.

Bob faced his dying with a gusto similar to the ample supply he had called upon for living. After many of us would have retreated from the world, he was still making final trips to see family and friends, and talking quite frankly about his approaching death. One day, only a few weeks before he did indeed die, four of us were discussing that prospect with him. One asked if he were considering chemotherapy.

"With this great head of hair?" he grinned. "Not on your life. You think I want to be bald and ugly when I die?" He was making a joke, as was his custom, but I think it was also a position statement, that death itself need not be ugly.

Perhaps that is what Meg saw when she looked in the face of death and told her husband it was OK. Certainly it was the message I got from Bernard and Kanya-Matzen got from her longshoreman friend: there is more here than ugliness, it need not be feared.

Creative Impulses

Appearing in his own play, *The Imaginary Invalid*, Moliere was in the process of taking the burlesque oath to become a doctor when he suffered the convulsion that led to his death just hours later. Certainly it was not in any script, but it was all somehow fitting: the dialogue, the drama, the dying, and the connectedness with Moliere's creative life.

Creativity has always seemed an elusive quality to me. I play bad guitar and worse piano, and have rarely produced a drawing, a dessert or even a short story with which I was entirely pleased. So the idea of a connection between the creative impulse and fearless dying began in my mind as sort of a double threat: it probably doesn't exist, but if it does, it is probably available only to the true artist. Not so. I believe it is more likely that creative impulses are a part of the human package. And if we have them as we come into the world, it stands to reason we may call on them as we go out.

Certainly the noted photographer Ruth Bernhard, whose graceful works are woven into the fabric of the twentieth century, exhibited a similar grace in some comments quoted in Michael Kenna's foreword to *Gift of the Commonplace*, a book of her still-life photographs published in her ninety-second year:

> "Dying is not a time for sorrow or sentiment," (Bernhard said, when asked about her future.) "It is a natural passing, a phase of existence. During our lifetime we should give everything away to those we come into contact with. Nothing is ever lost in the universe, it justs keeps turning over, and I am perfectly happy to turn over with it."

It has been immensely encouraging, for me, to discover that people of widely differing creative abilities seem able to put those skills to use in the simple art of dying, ranging from famous artists and writers to ordinary people known for an aspect of their extraordinary creativity. Their message seems to be that the creative impulse is available to humankind in the universal experience of dying just as it is in living.

An example is in the experiences of Keiko Mizushima, her husband Roger Keyes and their daughter, Aenea. Roger and Aenea speak of what was often a painful time as Keiko moved toward her dying; it became, though, a time of enlightenment for all three as well as for many of their friends.

Keiko Mizushima, the cherished only daughter of a university professor in Sendai, Japan grew up in the searingly difficult years of World War II and its aftermath. She enjoyed the unusual position, in a family of brothers, of favored child. Wanting his daughter to continue her education, Keiko's father sent her to International Christian University outside of Tokyo where she met Roger Keyes, an American who had grown up in the Philippines. They were not romantically involved but were immediately best friends, he says.

Roger finished his education at Harvard and began teaching in the U.S. Meanwhile, he helped arrange for Keiko to come to Sarah Lawrence College on full scholarship. Best-friendship did then grow into love, and in 1961 they married. A young woman of varied gifts, Keiko had studied music and creative writing at Sarah Lawrence, had played the violin since childhood and occasionally composed music. But she discovered her real passion almost accidentally. Noted California art dealer Ray Lewis, for whom Roger had been working, turned over his business to Roger and Keiko while he went to Europe for two years, and Keiko became fascinated with the ancient art of Japanese scrolls.

When Lewis returned, Keiko and Roger left for a year in Japan, where she studied scrolls and the ancient Japanese tradition of paper restoration. She was soon recognized in the U.S. as an expert in this intricate process. "It was partly her creative talent that made her so good at what she did," Roger says, "and partly a highly developed sense of craft." She worked successfully in her field while raising their daughter Aenea.

Keiko was first diagnosed with cancer in 1983. For the next five years she responded well to treatment, even though a new lump was discovered in the interim. With this second development, Keiko made changes in her lifestyle, sought alternative treatments and was optimistic about returning to health. For her fiftieth birthday in 1988, friends and family threw a big party, complete with a scrapbook of her life. Several days later she got the news that she had an inoperable cancer.

What followed, as described by Roger and Aenea, was an experience in learning both to connect and to disconnect. Keiko and Roger went together to a healer, and some combination of internal and external forces managed to shrink the tumor enough that Aenea left for a planned, extended trip to Bulgaria. Keiko decided that there was a connection between her work and her illness, and that she would need to extricate herself from her work, Roger says. "She wanted to separate from the driven, responsible self and let go of her current work, but on the other hand she recognized how important was her identity as a professional." Keiko knew she needed her identity as an artist but needed personal time even more. "So she made an orientational shift, to *being* rather than *doing,*" Roger explains. And like others in every stage of living and dying have done, she began to use visualization, calling on the images that had become familiar through her art: she would reject the war images, utilize the images of cliffs and winds, and doors. "It was like she was opening to the experience," Roger says.

Aenea Keyes was able to get back home before her mother died and later to play her violin at the memorial service. "I felt there was this doorway I could open now," she says; "that because I'd learned I was connected to something much larger than myself I could connect to others."

Another story, told by someone who was a lifelong friend of the subject, is more direct in showing a linkage between creative living and similar dying. His friend said I could call Marvin a hero. "He was just an ordinary person with extraordinary gifts that he used more gracefully than most of us. To me he was a hero."

Marvin, a 44-year-old Pennsylvania native who lived much of his adult life in Europe, used to say that in a previous life he was certain he had played the lyre in ancient Greece. A history teacher by trade, he loved playing his guitar or mandolin, or sitting down to anyone's piano; his friends say you never invited Marvin to a party unless you were prepared to hear him sing. So when he fell ill with leukemia no one was surprised that he turned to music for comfort.

"You could tell how Marvin was feeling when you walked in the door," one of his friends says. "Mozart, pretty good; Brahms, depressed; Grateful Dead, upbeat; Stravinsky, crazy with pain. But there was always music on; he said he couldn't get along without it."

The progression of Marvin's illness was quite fast. He underwent several different interventions, but after terrible experiences from side effects and facing the fact that there was little hope for recovery, he elected to stop almost all treatment except pain relief.

Marvin had been a churchgoer and choir singer, "but didn't consider himself very religious," his friend says. "When he knew he was dying and began to talk about it, he said, one day, 'You know who God is? God is the source of music. Who needs to know anything more? When I die, I'm going to return to the source of music'."

One night the friend stayed through the night with Marvin, who was getting noticeably weaker. All night long, the tapes played in the background, a mixture of classical music and swing from Marvin's specified selections. Early in the morning, Marvin called out to his friend.

"'Turn up the music,' he said, in this clear, precise voice. 'I want to listen very carefully',," the friend recalls. "It had been playing fairly softly, so I went over and turned it up. He just sort of smiled, then, and didn't say anything more. I thought he'd gone back to sleep, or into a coma or something. About fifteen or twenty minutes later he spoke again, almost as clearly as before although not as loud. 'You can turn the music down now,' he said, 'I can hear it from the source'." Less than an hour later, Marvin was dead.

If music was at the core of Marvin's life, art was at the core of Isabel Bishop's. The American realist painter and printmaker earned a prominent place as one of the leading women artists of the twentieth century.

Isabel Bishop moved from Detroit to New York in 1918 and began painting in a studio just off Union Square. She moved to a fourth floor studio overlooking the Square in 1934, and continued to capture the lives of the people she saw there until near the end of her long and productive life in 1988.

Bishop's figures are notable for communicating a sense of mobility and change, as if caught in a fleeting moment of conversation or action. The artist never felt any of her works reached a point at which they were "finished," writes Karl

Lunde in his 1975 monograph, but considered them "always work in progress, much like the people she paints." Lunde describes the painter herself as "of the moment and not of the moment."

Her friends found Bishop to be thoughtful and gentle behind her ever-observant eye, modest and self-deprecating; she was at home with many of the giants of twentieth century American art, but not with the brash or the self-congratulatory.

As she lay dying, Bishop was surrounded by a small group of friends who gathered around her to read poetry aloud and listen to her favorite music. She seemed to be enjoying the fellowship. At one point, she became as still as death itself, and a hush fell over the room. Then she opened her eyes again and said with a smile, "I was only teasing." Twenty minutes later, she did in fact make her final transition.

Another New York artist, Harriet Fitzgerald, founder of the Abingdon Square Painters, preceded Bishop in death by four years. Fitzgerald was on a painting trip to Italy with her long-time friend and fellow artist Peggy Anderson in the summer of 1984, in a part of the country where they often sought memorable scenes with which to fill their canvases. On July 3, they settled in on a flower-filled hillside near Castellina in Chianti where Fitzgerald created what would be her final painting. But she had already chosen another spot, a crucifixion scene at a little chapel at San Galgano, where she planned to set up her easel next. The little pieta intrigued her, Fitzgerald told Anderson, "because I think I have something to say about death."

The next morning, July 4, Anderson returned from an errand to find Fitzgerald had suffered a stroke. She was taken to the hospital in Sienna and eventually to a room looking out at the Sienna Cathedral. The friends rejected the idea of going to Rome, where more sophisticated life-support equiment might have prolonged Fitzgerald's days with a quality of life she had never wanted. She died on Bastille Day, July 14, leaving what she had to say about death, and life, in the vibrant paintings that survive.

British-born author Jessica Mitford, who had a lot to say about death as well as any number of aspects of life, called on the wit and unblinking wisdom that characterized her life and work when those were coming to a close. The indomitable author of *The American Way of Dying*, which helped change the face of the funeral business and many of our attitudes about dying, was never one to back off of an issue, whether the issue was social justice or her own mortality. She was also never one to miss out on the fun.

In the few times I saw her after we first met in 1993, what I thought most extraordinary was Mitford's ability to puncture pomposity in any form, to expose fraud and pretense, and to laugh throughout it all. Her memorial celebration, which I'm certain she would have enjoyed, was full of jokes and sometimes bawdy humor as well as testaments to what she accomplished while often employing those tactics. The artist Pele DeLappe, a friend of Mitford's since the early days of their involvement in leftist causes, served as mistress of ceremonies for the event, unceremoniously calling down those who went on too long. Anyone who committed one of the grammatical sins Mitford abhorred would also be loudly corrected.

Later, Mitford's daughter Dinky Romilly spoke of how her mother's wit and flair for the tongue-in-cheek dramatic continued into her dying. Summoning her grandchildren earlier than Romilly had planned to bring them from New York to California as her disease raged, Mitford said, "I want the whole deathbed scene."

Disdainful of her upbringing in upper class British society, Mitford fought all her life against class structure, against dogma and formality. Although she was supportive of young writers, and "uncritically accepting of her children and grandchildren," according to Romilly, Mitford absolutely could not tolerate the boring or the pompous. "Over the years, that sharp tongue sometimes turned even on her friends," Romilly recalls. "About someone terribly pedantic she would remark, 'I did not get the point of that person.' I used to say, 'You know, Mom, these people are not the class enemy'."

But it was that sharply critical eye and rapier wit that Mitford brought to bear in the writings, speeches and activities with which she profoundly affected her time. Timidity would not have worked.

Along the way, Mitford had been a heavy smoker and heavy drinker, though Romilly says her work was never affected by either. She gave up smoking some six or seven years before her death. About a year and a half before her death she also gave up drinking, after breaking her leg in a fall while on a visit to Romilly's home.

"After that," her daughter recalls, "it was almost miraculous how the unpleasant edge fell away. She became almost sweet." (But she "never became less radical, as many do when they get more comfortable.") While it is hard to visualize the zealous crusader as "sweet," it is not hard to see the interplay of creative forces that were a part of her dying and were celebrated at her memorial.

"One of the things about the end of her life," Romilly recalls, "is that she was symptom-free until almost right before she died. She experienced her first symptom on June 21, was diagnosed on July 3 and died on July 23."

Mitford faced the information about her diagnosis as she had faced so many other issues that needed to be dealt with: "absolutely head-on, no equivocating," Romilly says. She had two goals: to finish the book on which she was working (a revised new edition of her noted *American Way of Dying*, later completed by her widower Robert Treuhaft) and to make a previously planned trip to Cape Cod. When it quickly became evident that these goals could not be met, Mitford focused instead on "the whole deathbed scene," on confronting her dying and saying goodbye. "She told several of us, 'You know, it's actually good to know you are dying, because then you can make all your plans'."

Mitford's children and grandchildren came, and friends like poet Maya Angelou came, and there was the saying of goodbyes and singing of songs. In the process, Angelou changed some of the words. The ever-critical Mitford caught the changes, but in what would be one of her final judgments on the passing scene she indicated her approval of Angelou's revisions.

Richard Scott's creative gifts were more visual than literary. Scott, a California native who died in 1994, had spent his life making pictures, as a photographer and film editor. With his dying he brought into play all of the skills he had honed and lessons he had learned.

Not long after he turned fifty, Scott began to have physical troubles centering around back pain. He was just shy of his fifty-third birthday when the root of the troubles was diagnosed as pancreatic cancer, a form of the disease particularly virulent and resistant to treatment. The father of five grown children, Scott was deeply committed to both family and career and in no way ready to interrupt a richly rewarding life. Says his wife Mattie, "He just plain didn't want to go."

So, like fellow-Californian Jessica Mitford, Richard Scott met his destiny head-on. The Scotts lived in Berkeley, home of the University of California they had both attended (they had been high school sweethearts before then.) After his diagnosis, Richard went to the university bookstore, bought a large notebook and emblazoned its cover with a defiant 'C', clutched by the mascot California bear—only this C was for cancer and the bear a representation of Richard's own fighting spirit. Inside the notebook he began to compile instructions and information about his disease. In the front pages, he started a collection of quotations that helped express his philosophy of living and dying. One, from the thirteenth century Chinese philosopher Wu-Men, was a picture-image that would be at the top of the collection his family gave to friends at Scott's memorial service:

> One instant is eternity,
> > eternity is now.
> When you see through this one instant,
> > you see through the one who sees.

"Richard was a non-macho man," Mattie says. "I think that goes along with creativity. He was a faith-filled person—

using a combination of eastern meditation and regular Christianity—who believed that the whole of creation is so much more elegant than we can possibly imagine, that nothing disintegrates, it only changes."

Richard lived a little more than a year after his diagnosis. While worried about the film job he was struggling to complete he turned to another medium for making pictures: watercolor. On his 54th birthday, the week before he died, Mattie gave him a new box of colors. "He was a process-oriented person," she says. If it was the laying out and mixing of colors to achieve just the effect he wanted in the process of picture-making, or if it was the equally complicated process of dying, Richard wanted to be a part of it. Over those last days and weeks, he continued interweaving the two.

Though they had planned for him to die at home, Richard wound up back in the hospital the last few days of his life in an attempt to adjust pain medication. Family and friends came, and four of their five children. Son Paul had taken a teaching job in Japan a short time before, but had caught a plane for California when word came that his father was dying. When Mattie, trying to ease the sorrow of Paul's absence, told Richard their son was on his way, Richard gently contradicted her. "No, Paul is here," he said. "Paul is right here."

Mattie had a cot placed next to Richard's bed, so she could hold his hand through the night. "I would tell him," she says, "to keep looking toward the light, keep opening to the light." Richard's light had been from the sky he captured in his watercolors as much as through the lens of a camera, and from the eclectic blend of Christianity and eastern religions that sustained him.

Richard had relaxed, seemingly pain-free, after a group of friends gathered in the room and sang some of his favorite spirituals along with the rest of the family. He had painted his last picture, a choir he said was singing the anthem built on the words of the apostle Paul, "Eye has not seen, nor ear heard . . . the things which God has prepared for them that love him." But during the night he would periodically sit up in bed and give instructions about sound, or range, instructions familiar to Mattie because she had frequently worked with him on filmmaking projects.

"It was as if," she says, "he were making a video of his dying."

No one can say whether Richard Scott was indeed using familiar creative skills to participate in the final phase of his life or whether Jessica Mitford was critiqueing her own departure, if Keiko Mizushima found a connection between two realities or Michael found the source of his music. What we *can* say is that some creative individuals show us ways to do such things. Ruth Bernhard is one, Alexander Graham Bell was another and James Michener still another.

Credited with the invention of the telephone and a wide range of other signficant contributions to mankind, Bell was passionate about his work as a teacher of the deaf. It was through this work that he met his future wife, Mabel Hubbard, an early private student of Bell's. According to his biographer James Mackay *(Alexander Graham Bell)*, neither the passion for such teaching nor his devotion to Mabel ever wavered. When he died at the age of seventy-five in 1922, Bell's last words were an assurance to his wife that he would never leave her. They were given in sign language.

Michener, whose novels swept grandly through centuries and continents, left these parting words to his fans after learning of his final illness: "I approach this sad news with regret, but not with any panic. I savor every memory as they parade past. What a full life they made. And what a joy they bring me now. It is in this mood that my final days are passed."

Such final days leave little room for fear.

The Spirit of Laughter

As comedian Stan Laurel lay dying in February, 1965, shortly after a massive heart attack, he beckoned the nearby nurse to his side.

"I'd rather be skiing than doing this," Laurel said.

"Oh, do you ski, Mr. Laurel?" she asked.

"No," he replied; "but I'd rather be doing that than this."

Most of us would agree with that opinion of dying; not all of us would be able to joke about it at such a time.

Is it possible that laughter, the best medicine for living, may also be good medicine for dying unafraid? I think so. It may be hard to find anything light-hearted, let alone laughable, about one's dying moments; but when it happens the dying certainly seems to come easier.

As a child in rural and small-town Virginia during the 1940s the dying I saw came hard. Rooms were darkened, voices were hushed and somber, black suits came out of mothballs in readiness for funereal times ahead. My grandmother had dark blue dresses, reserved strictly for the occasion it seemed to me, which she wore when someone in the house was severely ill or dying. These were topped with plain aprons; the ones with flowers or ruffles stayed in the drawer. There was something about opposite conditions surrounding someone who was dying—lights, music, color, laughter—that implied disrespect, and being disrespectful was a cardinal sin of my childhood.

Yet laughter, not gloom, stands for much that one should particularly need to go about the business of dying. While symbolic of the things one is leaving behind—health and happiness, youthful abandon, perhaps—laughter also signifies strength and freedom. And it is the universal communication among humans, a possible last link with this world before stepping alone into another. None of those suggestions were acceptable in the dying I saw as a child.

So I was long grown when, on meeting Caroline as she lay dying, I first saw the possibility that laughter and dying might make appropriate bedfellows. For Caroline this was natural, because laughter was her nature.

Caroline was frail but wiry, an active black woman in her fifties when suddenly crippled by a massive stroke. Unable to care for herself and without family or resources, she wound up in county-subsidized Mountain View Rest Home near Atlanta where I often spent time singing with the residents, writing cards or playing games.

Caroline got pneumonia not many months after she arrived at Mountain View, and it was clear she had little chance of surviving. But she kept right on doing what she had always done best: laughing. She spoke of her impending demise as "going to meet my Maker," and that, for Caroline, was a laughing matter.

"You're bringing me that awful soup again, like that's gonna give me strength to meet my Maker? Honey, just take it right back." She would wave away an unwanted tray with a weak hand and a small grin. "He don't want me sloshing around heaven smellin' like watery collard greens." So she would have strong tea and a few slices of toast instead, while we got birthday cards ready for someone to mail to her friends, "after I go to meet my Maker."

On what turned out to be Caroline's last month on earth I saw her several times, often laughing at some new thing: a picture drawn by local school children, someone in the next room who had put her shirt on backwards. Once she told me she had seen Jesus a few nights earlier. "I think he's coming for me," she said, "and Lord, I don't want to be in this ragged old nightgown!" So we got two brand new cotton nightgowns for Caroline, and she laughed and said, "Am I gonna be a *sight* in those ribbons, going to meet my Maker."

Caroline died in the early morning of a sun-soaked June day, dressed in a be-ribboned nightgown but before she had had her tea or gotten her hair combed. Whoever came to pick her up for that long-awaited meeting with her maker must surely have found Caroline fussing over some fancied unreadiness but laughing, anyway, over the prospect of the journey.

Oscar Wilde, whose nineteenth-century journeys were light years away from the roads that Caroline traveled, left behind more than a few memorable comments. It was Wilde who reportedly said, on learning of an exorbitant fee for a surgical operation, "Ah, well, then, I suppose that I shall have to die beyond my means."

By the time he actually *was* dying, Wilde's capacity for humor must have worn thin. What with losing an ill-advised lawsuit and a worse one that followed, being imprisoned for homosexual practices and losing both reputation and long-time homeland, neither life nor death should have seemed a laughing matter any more. But the story persists that as he lay dying Wilde stared at the unlovely wallpaper of his room and remarked, "One of us must go."

Wilde's reported comment is one more *bon mot* that is exemplary of another enviable attitude most of us would like to claim. We are more likely to identify, though, with the phrase that most of us *have* used, "It only hurts when I laugh."

It is admittedly hard to laugh at pain. But some of the people I have known, and people I came to know through their stories, have called successfully on their ability to laugh to ease the pain of their dying. I believe that was true for Daniel (chapter 6), making a joke about his drug-laced fatal pudding, and for Bob (chapter 9), kidding about refusing chemotherapy so he wouldn't "die bald and ugly."

Humor is much more, though, than laughing out loud. A good sense of humor has proved an invaluable asset to countless mortals going through hard times, and seems to be equally valuable in that hardest of times, the time of dying. Southern California attorney Lloyd Smith spent long hours in his later years writing legal arguments for an individual's right to refuse life-prolonging treatment in terminal cases. When his own final illness came, Smith was emphatic about his readiness to die, refusing food to hasten that point. But he kept his sense of humor. A man who had long before rejected organized religion, when asked his religious preference during a last hospital admission, Smith replied, "Mozart."

Opal McCawley had endured enough to obliterate the most stalwart sense of humor by the time of her death in Knoxville, Tennessee in 1996. Opal experienced three decades of physical pain and disfigurement, alternately expecting to die within a matter of weeks and finding herself with renewed health and hope. In the years following her initial bout with breast cancer in 1964 she underwent twenty-seven surgeries. The first was a double radical mastectomy that was then a preferred treatment option; later occurrences of her cancer led to amputation of her right arm and a portion of her shoulder.

"Her odds were always no odds," says daughter Camille Williamson. "But she had a sense of humor, and a great faith."

Opal had married William James (Bill) McCawley, a minister and biology teacher, in 1939. Together they raised two daughters and a son, retired to Florida and continued to care for each other into their late eighties despite Opal's physical problems. But by the summer of 1996, with Bill's health also failing, their son Michael moved them to his home in Knoxville so that he could take a more active part in their care.

Shortly before Thanksgiving of that year, Bill fell and broke his hip. Opal, meanwhile, suffered congestive heart failure and at one point they were on the same floor of the local hospital, in different rooms. "I think when she realized he wasn't coming home she lost her own will to live," son Michael says. "While they were in the hospital a few rooms apart, though, I arranged to wheel her into his room so they could say goodbye." They did not speak, at that meeting, about Bill's oft-repeated wish to be cremated and have his ashes placed in Opal's coffin. He had given those instructions for his own funeral arrangements.

The family faced their mother's imminent death and began preparing for long-term convalescent care for their father. He was moved into a convalescent home, his bed placed beside a sunny window. Looking back, though, their children think the two had no intention to be separated for long. As she lay dying, with her family around her, Opal pointed to the end of her room and said of Bill, " I can see him right beside the window, looking at the flowers." When her oldest daughter remarked, "He's just waiting around for you," Opal motioned toward her long-absent arm and said, "Well, I'll just take this hand I don't have and go get him."

Opal died on Friday afternoon, December 27. With the family wrapped up in preparations for a Sunday morning memorial service, no one took time to go to the convalescent home the next day to break the news to Bill. As it turned out, such notification was never needed. Early Sunday morning a convalescent home nurse called to say she had gone to make a routine check and found he had died in his sleep.

"We were so much in awe of how they pulled it off," says daughter Camille, "that we were laughing and crying at the same time." The memorial service was expanded to include the two of them. Plans for Opal's burial in the family plot in Texas were delayed and Bill's cremated remains were placed inside the casket. Their children continue to believe that Opal's final quip was something more than a joke.

Laughter is a universal means of communication: a South Sea Islander and a Copenhagen businessman may not be able to exchange words, but if one laughs the other immediately gets a glimpse of what is meant. So it seems at least possible that it could be a communication between the known and the unknown.

Similarly, the kind of humor that enables us to connect with each other, to laugh at ourselves and our human condition or to chuckle over hard times long past can play a vital part in the dying process. It was this gentling kind of humor that was the particular gift of my beloved mother-in-law, Isabel Johns.

After her husband died, Isabel continued to live in the house they had bought in Detroit when he retired in the 1960s. It was the first house they had ever owned, moving as they had through a succession of Methodist parsonages during his nearly forty-year career as a Michigan minister. That immaculate two-story brick and frame home was the center of Isabel's world. I used to joke about how you could eat scrambled eggs off the floor, but it was no exaggeration. Every inch of space, every corner cupboard, drawer and shelf was so lovingly tended as to create a sense of order and tranquility I have seldom known at any other place or time.

When Isabel had a fall in May of 1996, shortly after her ninety-third birthday, it sent her into the hospital for one of the rare times she was ever away from her home space. The search for the cause of her fall led to discovery of colon cancer, which led to an operation she sailed through with customary determination—all ninety pounds of her. There was one explanation: Isabel wanted to get back home.

By mid-June, she was in a rehabilitation facility building up her strength and working toward that single goal. When I visited there I found her up to the task of trying to laugh at her fate. She could also smile with compassion at the other patients, some decades younger than she was, who protested over their therapies. And she could make small jokes, albeit half-hearted ones, about the lukewarm coffee and ice-cold room temperatures at the rehabilitation facility. Early in the morning of my last day I sneaked into the dark hallways and delivered a thermos of steaming coffee from her own coffee pot before I left for the airport, the two of us whispering like a couple of school children breaking curfew. At the end of that month my daughter and son-in-law visited, piling the great-grandchildren into the wheelchair with her for an outing on the grounds that produced laughing pictures in the sunshine.

An infection sent her back to the hospital the next week. Because the transportation vans were off duty on July 4, making it impossible for her to be taken back to the rehab facility that day, we had a long Detroit-San Francisco telephone visit during the afternoon. She talked about getting back to her house. My husband and I told her we had plane reservations to come and help her move in two weeks.

I was working, at the time, on a story about darning. It led us into a long, hilarious conversation about how many holes in how many socks she figured she had darned during the lean, depression-era years of her husband's low-paying job and her son's rambunctious childhood. In a decidedly unscientific calculation of that work, we came up with a probable average of twelve holes per week, for a lifetime total of some twenty thousand repair jobs. Isabel would periodically abandon the calculations, then come right back with a small laugh and another reminiscence: " . . . and then there were the holes in the elbows of sweaters . . . "

A few hours after we hung up the phone, another call came to say she had simply, quietly, fallen asleep and died. I told my husband I thought that it must have done her in, the remembrance of all that hard work over all those years. I think Isabel would've enjoyed the joke. Comfortable with the notion that she was indeed headed home, I think she also enjoyed the laughter of those final hours.

My friend Ed Currie, who died of AIDS in 1996, could be caustic, wry or funny, and occasionally all three at the same time.

Ed had been a college professor and a corporate executive. He was good at taking charge and giving orders, not good at suffering fools or beating around the bush. When a new minister paid a call during the early stages of his illness, Ed greeted him at the door with characteristic candor. "Okay," he said, "let's cut the BS. You tell me where you're coming from and I'll tell you what's going on with me."

Toward the end of his life the neuropathy that caused pain in Ed's feet was one of the things that troubled him most. His daughter Lisa and I were among those approved for giving foot rubs. I would sometimes ask, after I'd done what I considered a particularly good job, if he felt any better. "Well, you're not as good as Lisa," he would say. Then he'd crack a suggestion of a smile. "But keep at it. You'll improve."

I never did approach Lisa's level and Ed, unfortunately, didn't improve either. But in those terrible last days it was his humor that carried us all through. I think it carried him through as well.

I don't know anyone who has felt that dying itself had any element of humor about it. However staunch, however full of faith or possessed of a sense of readiness, I doubt that anyone looks on her own dying—or anyone else's, for that matter—as something to laugh about. What I do believe is that those who see humor in the human condition, and who see dying as *part* of the human condition, can sometimes make a correlation between the two. And it may help carry us through. It undoubtedly helped two whose stories appear in chapter 10: Jessica Mitford, making cracks about "wanting the whole deathbed scene," or Isabel Bishop, playing a parting joke on her friends with the comment, after seeming to be dead, "I was only teasing."

None of these incidents, relating as they do to the lives we live, trivialize the final moments of those lives. Rather, they seem to me a graceful way of living through those moments. Surely laughter, the universal communication, need not be confined to this small, capricious corner of the universe.

Who's in Control Here?

Loss of control has to be right up there with loneliness or unremitting pain as the thing that strikes terror to my heart. I would divulge any secret to the enemy just to avoid being thrust onto a roller coaster, unable to apply brakes or flatten the course for four or five minutes. I strongly resist even sensible plans forced on me by others. And a major benefit of sobriety is, for me, avoiding the helplessness of being unable to have words or feet precisely at my command. I think I am not alone in preferring to retain control of my time and circumstances.

So how terribly frightening it must be to die. To relinquish all control of everything one has and loves and is, and surrender oneself to the unknown. That, at least, is the thought behind the nagging dread I associated with dying for many years.

But another perspective is suggested by those who retain control, sometimes against overwhelming odds, of their dying. As if by claiming ownership of their dying moments they symbolically walk through death's door under their own power. To walk through death's door that way is, it certainly seems, to do so unafraid.

New Jersey opthalmologist Anne Ricks Sumers' brother Rick managed to do so, against *truly* overwhelming odds. But Rick had fought against overwhelming odds for years. He survived a brain tumor at eighteen, went on to finish college and law school, marry, have a son and embark on a successful career. When he was still a young man, having undergone three separate brain surgeries with each carrying the risk of being left in a vegetative state, having had his cancerous kidneys removed and subsequently picked up living once more while on dialysis, he knew what he wanted: life with reasonable quality or to die at home

"Rick was only forty, a nice, funny guy, a good husband, a dedicated lawyer, a father of a little boy who needs him," Sumers wrote in a *Newsweek* essay published shortly after her brother's death. "He didn't 'choose death'; he wanted desperately to live, but a brain tumor was killing him and the doctors couldn't do a thing. He had only one choice: die in the hospital or die at home."

In a telephone conversation about a year after her essay appeared, Sumers told me of the mixed emotions experienced by friends and family throughout her brother's illness, and of the strength of will he demonstrated. "We (friends and family) were not at peace, we were feeling it was gross unfairness," she says. "Of the five stages of grieving, we were pretty much stuck in anger. But we helped him do the last thing he wanted and we were able to say, 'This is a good thing we have done'."

Her brother's final days, Sumers says, arrived without warning and with stunning speed. One day he seemed confused, the next he was hallucinating and the following day an MRI showed his brain studded with inoperable cancer. The best doctors could offer was to buy a few more weeks of life with chemotherapy. But all Rick wanted was to go home, a desire he repeated in all of his lucid moments.

Rick's humor returned, intermittently, Sumers says, along with his lucidity. Told at one point that things were really bad, he asked, *"How* bad?" And when the response came, "Your brain is full of cancer," he replied, "You could've sugar coated it a little."

In her *Newsweek* essay Sumers wrote, "Rick was confused and disoriented, but he was fully aware that he was confused and disoriented. I showed him pictures of my children I keep on my key chain; he shook my keys and gently put them back in my hand: 'You better drive. I'm too f---ed up to drive.' But he begged to go home."

Though there was too little time to arrange for Hospice care, Rick's wife was determined he should have his wish. Within two hours of the family's decision that he should leave the hospital, he was in an ambulance on his way to his house in Washington. Once inside, he immediately relaxed.

"Rick's last evening was wild, fun, tragic and exhilarating," Sumers wrote. "Rick walked from room to room in his house, savoring a glass of red wine, eating a cookie, talking with his best friend, our mother and dad, our sisters and brothers. Neighbors stopped in with food and stayed for the conversation. Friends from the Quaker Meeting House stopped by. Cousins arrived.

"It was like Thanksgiving—good food, lots of conversation; but the guest of honor would be dead in a few days, or hours.

"Although Rick was confused he wasn't frightened. Rick knew he was in his home, surrounded by friends and family. He was thrilled to be there. He ate. He cleaned. He was busy all evening, reminiscing, telling fragments of stories, neatening up, washing dishes, giving advice and eating well.

"At the end of the evening he brushed his teeth, washed his face, lay down in his wife's arms in his own bed and kissed her goodnight. By morning he was in a deep coma.

"All that long Saturday my family was together and we grieved. We watched over Rick. My father planted bulbs, daffodils and tulips, to make the spring beautiful for his grandson. My mother washed Rick's hair. My brothers and sisters and in-laws painted the porch banisters. Family, friends and neighbors came by to see him sleeping in his bed. Sometimes as many as ten people were in his bedroom, talking, crying, laughing or telling stories about him, or just being with him—other times it was just his wife.

"He took his last breath with his wife and his best friend beside him, his family singing old folk songs in the living room. He was peaceful, quiet, never frightened or restrained."

Sumers maintains that the choice of where and how he would die was the only matter left over which her brother had control at the end of his life. The alternative he had experienced: tied down by hospital staff because he kept getting out of bed he was "furious, humiliated, embarrassed, enraged, confused and frightened." But in making that final decision to go home she believes Rick and his wife, his doctors and family made possible the kind of dying he sought. "Rick died far too young," she wrote. "But everyone should hope to die like this; not just with dignity, but with fun and love, with old friends and family."

In a different manner, my friend Alphonso Sloop retook control of his life in the days of his dying.

If there has ever been anyone who was universally loved, it was Alphonso. He was not a saint, he was simply someone who loved humankind without reservation and invited humankind to love him back. Alphonso had one of those instantaneous grins, under a lush handlebar mustache, that was so irrepressible and contagious when he flashed it at you it was virtually impossible not to dissolve into merriment, even if you'd been angry with him three minutes earlier. He and his grin were like one of those jack-in-the-box clowns. Fate would smash the top down hard, only to have a laughing face pop back up. Alphonso was a landscape gardener, a tenor, a crusader for truth and justice, an indiscriminate hugger and a lover of life. Like Rick, he died far too young.

Fighting simultaneously against cancer and AIDS, Alphonso was in and out of hospitals several times in that last year. As it happened, I had stopped by for a visit during one such hospitalization just as he was meeting with his doctor to discuss the future. He asked that I stay. The interventions for his cancer, which was rapidly progressing, had been buying him time but making him miserable.

"I have decided," Alphonso told the doctor (a young man who was himself battling cancer), "to go off the chemo." All three of us knew that meant he would die quite soon.

"OK," said the doctor, "you can go on home today." Then he did something that seemed to me a credit to the profession of medicine. "What do we doctors know?" he asked. "Your body could take over and you could do just fine for a matter of days or weeks, or possibly even months. You could die at any moment; you could live for a while feeling better than these past few days. Or you can change your mind tomorrow." Alphonso smiled and said, "That's true."

So he packed his duffel bag and left the hospital. He did not change his mind. In the few weeks that followed he worked on putting his affairs in order, went to the movies, and lent his smiling presence to the final hours of a dying friend. Friends and family came. I traded him bowls of soup for his lemon squares recipe. There were expressions of love and affection emanating from his house like ripples on a quiet lake. And then he was gone. We followed his instructions for a memorial service, which featured the whole church choir and a harp solo—and I believe the spirit of those days immediately before and after his death was a testament to the fact that Alphonso took back the control of them all.

Taking control of the end of one's life is, of course, no new idea. Everyone who self-delivers does just that, and many of the stories in other chapters are essentially stories of taking, or keeping control. It is a common literary theme of fact and fiction, as eloquently demonstrated in books like Anna Quindlen's *One True Thing* or Mitch Albom's *Tuesdays With Morrie*. "If Professor Morris Schwartz taught me anything at all," Albom wrote, "it was this: there is no such thing as 'too late' in life. He was changing until the day he said good-bye."

Similar instances of keeping control, of living into one's last moments, abound in novels, plays and short stories. And there are equally eloquent stories in history. One such is the story of William Sydney Porter, known to history as the storyteller O. Henry.

Born in Greensboro, North Carolina in 1862 as the Civil War raged around his family, Porter spent his first few decades weathering an assortment of shifting fates largely through the support and rescue efforts of his friends and eventually his in-laws. But he learned about absolute loss of freedom and control during a three-year prison term for misappropriation of bank funds at the turn of the century. It was during this time that the pseudonym "O. Henry" came into being, along with Porter's feverish struggle to conceal his past and to keep his true identity secret from the fans and associates who emerged with his growing fame. That struggle, along with what seems to have been a losing battle with alcoholism, shaped the few years that remained of his life.

As he collapsed in his New York apartment on June 3, 1910, writes biographer Richard O'Connor in *O. Henry*, Porter managed to call a friend who in turn summoned Dr. Charles Hancock. Hancock wanted to call for an ambulance, but Porter insisted on leaving under his own power, dressed and combed and maintaining, during the taxi ride to the hospital, "a gentlemanly sense of obligation ingrained to the marrow of his character . . . (chatting) with Dr. Hancock as though they were on their way to dinner at Rector's instead of hurrying by taxi to the hospital.

"At the hospital's emergency entrance he again insisted on walking without assistance," O'Connor writes. "When the reception clerk asked for his name, he replied: 'Call me Dennis. My name will be Dennis in the morning.'

"His friends believed that he entered the hospital under an assumed name because he didn't want any publicity, but actually it was consistent with his view of himself as a man living underground. Finally he decided that his name should go on the hospital records as 'Will S. Parker'," O'Connor reports, at least the given name and initials with which he began his journey through fact and fiction.

At midnight on June 4, as the lights in his room were dimmed, Porter said, "Turn up the lights. I don't want to go home in the dark." He died early the following morning, O'Connor relates, "not in the dark, but with the dawn light streaming through the window."

Elements of control over our final days are outside the reach of most of us. We can't all spend them surrounded by loved ones, and we certainly can't dress for a taxi ride to the hospital emergency room—and then have the same doctor at our pleasant bedside (as Dr. Hancock was at Porter's) twenty-four hours later. What we can do is look at the ways in which others have kept control and what that seems to have meant. Their stories can also have meaning for us.

Private Choice, Public Dilemma

Try this: Close your eyes, squeeze them shut tight if you want, and imagine you are in what you know to be the last few weeks, or perhaps months, of this life. Now imagine you are in terrible pain which seems beyond relief or are suffering indignities you had never imagined, and you are helpless to change those circumstances.

Now ask yourself this question: If you had the option of having a physician whom you trusted assist you with the drugs which would bring death sooner, rather than later, would you make that choice?

It is a question with no easy answers, but one worth pondering. Perhaps you have religious convictions which prevent your pondering it for long, or at all. Or you may have a stumbling block such as the prospect of leaving someone you love feeling betrayed. There are countless stumbling blocks in the way of an answer to this question, but it is still one that merits a continuing struggle.

When the question gets tangled up in the broader issues of legalizing physician-assisted dying, or when you start thinking about someone *else* making such a choice for you, the complexities quickly grow. What guarantees that the choice is being made while the chooser is in his or her right mind? Who decides what being in one's right mind even is? What kind of safeguards can be established and maintained?

But come back to the personal question and take an honest look. The issue is not new and absolute honesty has not always played a major role in related discussions. Countless physicians today will admit, privately, that they have given a little extra morphine to some suffering patient already at the doorway to death. Some swear they have not and would not do so, but say they would still want that choice for themselves.

One who wanted that choice, and made it for himself, was Sigmund Freud. Long after the time when he had written his friend Oskar Phister of his determination not to outlive the capacity for orderly thought (and long before such a thing was a matter of public discussion), Freud made a pact with his own physician, Max Schur. The agreement was that Schur would hasten Freud's death when the appropriate time (in Freud's opinion) came.

That time came after a long battle with cancer. It was in 1939 in London, the city to which Freud had fled from his Vienna home just over a year earlier. Biographer Peter Gay records Freud's comment to Schur, who was at his bedside: "Schur, you remember our 'contract' not to leave me in the lurch when the time had come. Now it is nothing but torture and makes no sense."

Schur indicated that he had not forgotten, Gay writes. "Freud gave a sigh of relief, kept (Schur's) hand for a moment, and said, 'I thank you.' Then, after a slight hesitation, he added, 'Talk it over with Anna (Freud's daughter), and if she thinks it is right, then make an end of it'."

Following three injections of morphine over a period of hours, Freud lapsed into a coma on September 22, dying at 3 a.m. the next morning. "The old stoic," Gay writes, "had kept control of his life to the end."

Keeping control. It is precisely that which is at the heart of many stories in other chapters and it is at the heart of the issue for most of those wanting to see physician-assisted dying made legal in this country. But sixty years after completion of the "contract" between Freud and Schur, the issue of physician-assisted dying is no longer just a matter between patient and doctor. It is instead a very public issue seen in the cold and ever-shifting light of its complex moral, legal and ethical implications. Try to strip all of those away, and take yourself back to the private question: would you want that choice for yourself?

Several years ago, a man in his late fifties was facing certain death from AIDS. He lived in Seattle, Washington, where he had a host of friends and a strong support system. What he did not have was hope.

One night he left home, alone, made his way to a roadway overpass, and leapt to his death on the pavement below.

At almost the same time, there was a woman in a Northern California city who was wheelchair-bound, dying painfully of cancer. She too had friends and support; her husband looked after their needs and had professional help so that she could remain at home.

The attached garage of the couple's ranch-style suburban home was on a level with the room where the woman often stayed while her husband was gone. When he returned from work one afternoon he called the emergency squad to say he had found his wife in the driveway, dead. No one at first could figure out what happened. But later in the county morgue, where the woman's body had been taken, the unmistakable signs of carbon monoxide poisoning began to emerge, and with them the real story:

Desperate to put an end to what she saw as intolerable suffering for herself and her family, the woman had dragged herself, on her elbows, into the garage, managed to start the car and bring her life to an end. Because they were devout Catholics, her distraught husband had sought to avoid the censure of family, friends and church by moving her body into the driveway.

These stories, widely differing in their details, had the same effect: they mobilized efforts to seek a change in the laws prohibiting physician-assisted dying.

"He should not have had to die alone, or to die so violently," says Susan Dunshee of her friend in Seattle. Dunshee, the Director of the Seattle AIDS Support Group, became a founder and later board chairman of an organization called Compassion in Dying. Within a few years that small, financially limited but passionately committed group had led the first successful challenge to a law prohibiting physicians from assisting terminally ill persons who seek to hasten their own death. It is now a national non-profit association, Compassion in Dying Federation of America.

Charlotte Ross speaks of the California woman's agonizing death in explaining her own commitment to a similar organization, Death with Dignity National Center. Ross, now the Center's Executive Director, came into this particular job after a distinguished career in suicide prevention. Like most others seeking change in an increasingly controversial area, it is life which she cherishes, not death.

"In 1965," Ross recalls, "I learned that a favorite college professor had committed suicide. I wondered how, in the midst of all that bright, well-informed community, such a thing could happen. This was ten years after the first suicide-prevention chapter had been formed there, but when I went to the San Mateo Library I found a total of three books dealing with the subject."

Things are vastly different today. Thanks to the efforts of countless people who, like Charlotte Ross, have had their lives jolted by the suicide of a friend or family member, there are suicide hotlines through which teenagers can now get mental health counseling without parental consent, there are support groups for people of all ages and in all walks of life, and dozens of books offering guidance and help are on most library shelves.

Ross, along with many others, believes the issue of physician-hastened death calls out for similar attention. Reduced to a simple question, would you want that choice for yourself, the question still has no simple answer.

One person who made that choice, after intense soul-searching convinced her there was no other option, was a Virginia woman named Lona Jones, who ended her life in June 1996 with the assistance of "Dr. Death," Dr. Jack Kevorkian.

Lona Jones was a neuro-orthopedic nurse who had practiced her profession with a combination of kindness and skill for nearly forty years. At the same time she had raised two cherished daughters, volunteered in places like her church and local crisis centers, and constantly continued to study and update her skills.

When she was diagnosed with brain cancer eighteen months before she died, Lona Jones knew exactly what her prospects for the future were. She underwent a craniotomy, chemotherapy and radiation treatments in an effort to slow the progress of the disease. She knew she might buy some time, but had no illusions about the eventual course her cancer would take. Lona and her husband Ralph researched the subject from every possible angle and consulted with specialists at some of the best cancer centers in the country.

About a year after her initial diagnosis, though, Lona Jones began to face the fact that life, as she felt it worth living, was nearing an end. The things she had loved to do—drawing and wood-carving, cooking, decorating, entertaining friends, even the routine matters of shopping or driving a car—were no longer possible. A woman of deep religious convictions, she had no fear of dying; what she feared was the seizure that would take away her decision-making ability and therefore her control of her own choices. So she wrote to Dr. Kevorkian.

Lona did sound out some doctor friends, Ralph Jones says, "but she could not ask them to break the law. Stockpiling drugs went against her very nature; she was so honest she couldn't even rathole money from me without telling me about it before she actually went out and bought something she'd been saving for.

"The difficulty (of making that final trip to Michigan to die) was not in the ethics, theology or morality," Ralph Jones says now, "but in the timing of making a rational decision." For a period of months the couple talked with their daughters and exchanged letters, medical information and phone calls with Dr. Kevorkian.

In May 1996, Lona Jones knew her decision-making time was running out. She had had fourteen seizures that month, now affecting the entire upper portion of her body. Her ability to read—virtually the last life-enhancing activity left to her— was limited because of the attendant complications.

Ralph Jones does not talk about the specifics of how and where his wife, "my best friend for probably forty-five years," ended her life. They both knew the public perception of "Dr. Death," a man they nevertheless found to be "comforting, soothing and always emphasizing that his objective was to prolong her life as long as possible and that the decision was hers." They also knew that there would be friends who would feel betrayed, and people who would say their actions were wrong for a long list of reasons. But Lona Jones made that final choice she felt was hers to make. She and her husband booked a flight to Detroit in mid-June.

On June 20, Lona Jones was pronounced dead of carbon monoxide poisoning at the North Oakland Medical Center in Pontiac, Michigan, where she was taken on the last journey she would make with her best friend.

"Marjorie," was another woman who made such a choice with her own best friend, a physician. That physician, who did not want his name or Marjorie's real name used, told me of her death at the end of a long, painful struggle against lung cancer. "With Marjorie it was simply a matter of feeling she was unable to bear the pain and indignity any longer," her doctor says. "With me it was a matter of caring for her as long and as well as I could, and giving her final relief when she made it clear that was what she wanted. We drank wine and told stories, and I gave her an injection of morphine. It was an act of love, and a time of love."

Most physicians who talk of having assisted someone's death—and there are many—characterize it similarly, yet in every U.S. state except Oregon it is still against the law. When the Supreme Court in June 1997 refused to overturn such a law (challenges had been made to the laws prohibiting physician-hastened dying in New York and Washington) the legality was settled for now; but the issue is unlikely to go away. "We are disappointed but not discouraged," has been the operative phrase among those who brought the case to the Supreme Court, according to Barbara Coombs Lee.

Lee, now Executive Director of Compassion in Dying Federation of America, was formerly director of the Washington organization (mentioned above). Compassion in Dying was founded in April 1993 to provide personal help for dying patients who want to make informed decisions about their deaths—including decisions about hastening that moment. "It is not pain that usually motivates people to seek to hasten their dying," Lee explains. "It's more existential: loss of self. Pain can always be treated, if a person doesn't mind being unconscious.

What we see all the time are people not in denial but people who know clearly that their time is limited, and are asking, 'What do I want the quality of that time to be?' It's one of the most important questions, most important life tasks they face."

Lee names a few of the prominent people who have died recently, at home, with friends and family around, after a severe illness but without prolonged suffering and debilitation. She and others say with certainty that in many cases the attendant physician, acting on mutual agreement with the patient, hastened death. "But what if you don't have money and power?" she asks. "You can be denied the chance for your death to have meaning."

"Jane Roe" made certain her death had meaning. A Seattle physician who was herself dying of cancer, Roe was one of the four plaintiffs who challenged the Washington state law banning physician-assisted dying. She was in an unusual position to do so: she strongly believed that the time had come for her own life to end, yet she could not legally be assisted in hastening that end by her husband, himself a physician.

Jane Roe was an intellectual, a highly skilled, widely read woman with training and certification in several disciplines. She loved exploration and discovery, her husband says; "she would do everything necessary until she had a very clear sense of what might be a very complicated situation." She was also a compassionate woman who loved life.

And Jane Roe was intensely private. As her physical condition deteriorated she found herself in precisely the position Barbara Coombs Lee describes: unafraid of pain, but unwilling to prolong a life she felt needed to end. Then sixty-nine, and at the end of a twenty-year battle with breast cancer, she decided to leave a final legacy. From the bed on which virtual paralysis had kept her for months, Jane Roe videotaped a plea that she and other dying patients be allowed to hasten their deaths with the help of their doctors. Her husband believes the video was a key to the success of that initial court battle. Their winning decision was overturned, and the right of states to ban physician-assisted dying eventually upheld by the Supreme Court. Roe would probably also have been "disappointed but not discouraged."

Seattle cardiologist Tom Preston was one of the four doctors named as co-plaintiffs in the lawsuit filed on behalf of Jane Roe and two other dying patients. Preston argues that physicians too often participate in "prolonged, needless suffering, extreme therapy to eke out another few hours or days because they are unable to give up.

"Hippocrates," he adds, "never had a patient on a ventilator." Preston believes the laws banning physician-assisted dying need changing for a number of reasons. One is, he maintains, that such laws are widely disregarded anyway and the source of great ambivalence among doctors themselves. In a recent unscientific survey of Seattle physicians, Preston says, ninety per cent of those doctors said they would want the option of choosing assisted suicide for themselves and sixty-eight per cent would want that option open to their patients. But only fifty per cent said they would be willing to help hasten dying for a terminally ill patient themselves.

But Preston's strongest argument for change in the laws banning physician-hastened dying comes from his own experience with Compassion in Dying, on whose board he serves. "The people we have counseled who have died at home, surrounded by their loved ones," he says, "have had the most peaceful dying I've known. They have been able to have support, understanding and often reconciliation. The most moving case I can think of was a patient of mine whose wife flew up from Mexico, ending an estrangement that had lasted for twenty years."

Those who argue that the laws should remain make equally eloquent cases about the sanctity of life, the potential for abuse (if physician-hastened dying were legalized,) and the fact that pain can always be alleviated. It is certainly true that pain can always be alleviated, or at the least managed. It has been demonstrated, furthermore, that people wishing to die often change their minds when they are treated for depression. But easy answers do not fit the complexity of the question: would you want the choice for yourself?

Alice Hagli made her own choice about dying—and wound up living far beyond all expectations. I visited Alice in 1996 in the neat, smoke-filled living room of her mobile home in Lynnwood, Washington, a few months before her original death date. She had contacted Compassion in Dying long before then, knew she had the wherewithal to end her own life when she felt that time had come and knew she would not have to die violently, in pain or alone. With a tumor on her lung (which didn't deter her from the chain-smoking that almost wiped out this interviewer) and others elsewhere in her body, Alice chose not to undergo surgery or other interventions but instead to let her life run out its course.

"My mother died in 1971, and that's when I started thinking about all this," she said. "I'm absolutely terrified of pain. Why should they expect us to live in the hospital and suffer? My husband died four years ago of a rare form of cancer, after two sessions of chemo and radiation. I would drive him back and forth to the hospital five days a week. It was his body, and his choice."

Alice felt differently about her own choice, although it is difficult to believe it was motivated by her being "terrified" of anything. "I'm a Taurus, you know," she said, "the bull; I believe in grabbing the bull by the horns and nobody dares stop me. Especially on this, this is too personal. And I *know* there is a better place, that I'm going to get to see the people I love."

So Alice set her death date for the anniversary of her husband's death in October. The following spring I spoke with her Compassion in Dying volunteer Sheila Cook and was surprised to hear Alice was in fact still going strong. "It's not unusual," Cook told me. "We often find that when people know they don't have to worry about their dying they manage to go right on living, better, and sometimes longer."

Alice set about doing both. She flew to Alaska with the daughter from whom she had been estranged, visited friends on Hood Canal, and later went to her granddaughter's wedding. "I got a motel room, so I'd have a place for my daughter too; the reception was at that same motel. Neither of us could sleep that night, so we just got up and had a glass of sparkling cider.

"I'm a rebel at heart," Alice told me over the phone then (spring, 1997), with the same blunt assertiveness she'd demonstrated nearly a year earlier. "I don't like people making decisions for me. Oh, they can make suggestions, they just can't tell me what to do." So Alice, chain-smoking, refusing therapies and taking her own bulls by the horn to the end, repeatedly reset her death date until her life could run the course she believed had been its intended plan.

In September 1997, at the recommendation of her physicians, Alice went on Hospice care, which anticipated she had perhaps another six months to live at most. But I spoke with her once more in February 1998 and she said, "I think they're going to kick me off." The tumor on her lung was hardly any bigger than it had been the previous fall.

Asked how she was feeling at that point Alice said, "I get awfully tired—but what else is new? The Hospice nurse tried to get me on regular pain medication, something like the patch, but I said if I don't have that much pain, what's the use? Every once in a while I have a little hurt. When and if the pain gets to what I call unbearable, then I'll think about setting my death date again."

But in early 1998, two years after the diagnosis that indicated she would die very soon, Alice was still going strong, still chain smoking, and clearly enjoying being something of a poster woman for Compassion in Dying. I suggested she might want to stick around and read about herself in this book, and I sincerely hope she is doing exactly that.

Organizations like Compassion in Dying and the Center for Death Education can offer only information, support and the assurance that the client's dying will be as close as possible to what the individual wishes. Beyond that, physician-hastened dying remains an "underground" practice, unquestionably available to some and legally available to few in the U.S.

Reader's Digest contributing editor Eugene H. Methvin referred to some of the evidence of this practice in an article titled "A Compassionate Killing," which first appeared in the *Wall Street Journal* on January 20, 1997. Methvin cited the furor arising from publication of an anonymous article in the *Journal of the American Medical Association* in 1988 in which a doctor-in-training told of administering a lethal injection of morphine to a young woman dying of ovarian cancer.

"I asked my friend Dave Hubbard, a psychiatrist in Dallas, about the article," Methvin wrote. "Dr. Hubbard began practicing medicine as a teenager in the 1930s. His dad was a country doctor in New Mexico; sometimes, when busy at a patient's bedside, he would send Dave off to deliver a baby. Dave graduated from medical school just in time to go to war in the Pacific, and came home to take over the practice while his dad took a well-deserved vacation.

"The *JAMA* article and controversy didn't faze Dave. 'We used to think nothing about helping some old boy who was having a hard time quitting breathing on out,' he told me. 'It's easy. You just give 'em a big dose of morphine, and it depresses the breathing apparatus. Their breathing slows, and they just ease on out as peacefully as a baby going to sleep'."

That story took Methvin back more than thiry years. "I saw my mother, my brother and myself gathered at my father's bedside, on June 4, 1953," he wrote.

"Just past his fifty-fifth birthday, my father had spent long months wasting away from inoperable cancer. The surgeons had done an exploratory operation, taken one look and pronounced a death sentence. Today they would have removed the tumor, rooted in the aorta, and replaced the artery with a

Dacron substitute. Dad would have lived on. But in 1953 they said, 'about six months,' and it was almost exactly that.

"Dad was a lifelong newspaperman. He and Mother, his staunch co-editor, together had faced down pistol-toting sheriffs, defied the Ku Klux Klan lynchers and night-riders, and defeated courthouse pols bent on running them out of town. And early in their marriage they had agreed that before either would let the other endure a long, agonizing death, the partner would provide the means for the ailing one to make an end of it."

The time for such an action came, Methvin wrote, shortly after his father had finally had to give up going to the office every day. After a painful attack his mother called their family physician, Martin Malloy, who lived around the corner. "Dr. Malloy administered a shot of morphine to stop the pain. Then he said, 'Claude, don't worry about what's ahead. We're not going to let you suffer with this thing. We still have the heavy pain killers, and we're going to use them.'

"Dad slept most of the next day. After supper we sat together on the bedside and I reported on our progress with the week's edition. (Methvin had dropped out of college and gone to work at the family paper.) My older brother had come from his job in another town to help, and we expected to get our eight-page paper printed and to the post office by midnight.

"Brother and I had hardly gotten back to the newspaper when a neighbor telephoned. 'Gene, your mama says get home right away. It's your dad.' We met Dr. Malloy pulling up into the driveway and followed him to the bedside. Dad had gone into some sort of a seizure; he was gasping, glassy-eyed—a heart attack? After a brief examination and a shot in Dad's once-muscular arm, Dr. Malloy beckoned us into the living room. 'He's started hemorrhaging heavily in the stomach,' he said. 'This is what we've all known was coming. We could take him around to the hospital and give him transfusions and prolong it for a couple of days, but not longer,' he said.

"Together the three of us recoiled at the very thought of inflicting such pain and indignity on this man who was a hero to us all; we shook our heads emphatically. Dr. Malloy expected exactly such a response. He had been my parents' friend for decades; he knew of their feelings and agreement about terminal care. He didn't hesitate. 'Just give me a minute, and you can come back in,' he told us.

"When he summoned us, Dad's desperate gasping had already eased, and his eyes had closed. We sat by the bed, Mother, Brother and I, taking turns holding his hands. Over the next half hour, his breathing grew shallower and slower, subsiding into gentle sighs until finally, it drifted away entirely.

"Not until my 1988 conversation with Dave Hubbard did I understand that in those few moments before Dr. Malloy called us back, he had administered a lethal dose of morphine. I wondered why it had never occurred to me before, nor to my mother or brother," Methvin wrote. "For years afterward, knowing the terrible and prolonged suffering that some cancer patients endured, we had marveled that a merciful Providence had spared us such an ordeal. We did not realize how grateful we should have been to our family physician."

It is entirely probable that a half-century ago, when family physicians lived just around the corner and had been family friends for decades, such scenes were commonplace. In those earlier, simpler, pre-managed care, pre-litigiousness days, it is probable that the only question was, "Has the time come?"

Today, the question is a whole set of new questions: "Will I be thrown in jail? Will I burn in hell? Will somebody sue?" Those questions tend to overshadow the more pertinent questions: "Is this dying person's pain and indignity too great? Should life of this quality be prolonged? Should one's own wishes, in dying, be honored?"

The U.S. Supreme Court settled the overall issue for now with its June 1997 decision. That ruling upheld the laws of forty-nine states which prohibit physicians from helping their patients hasten death. Some cheered the decision, some lamented it; most people in those forty-nine states quite probably didn't notice. But the fact is that each one of us *will* die, and not all of us will do so as closely in compliance with our own wishes as Alice Hagli or Sigmund Freud or Claude Methvin.

The questions of how we live and how we die, with or without physician assistance, are a long way from being solved. But while people like "Jane Roe" or Alice Hagli or Eugene Methvin's father may have feared other things—pain of their own or their families, other complications, prolonged agonies—none of them feared dying. They were fortunate at least in having compassionate professionals in attendance who understood that fact.

Models

After all is *truly* said and done, can anyone claim it is possible to die unafraid, to confront death and make it one's own? I believe it is.

I have had people loudly, angrily dispute this belief. I have had people ask me who my "experts" are, or what gives me the right to assert such a notion. I have certainly had my own qualms about going public with this belief since I am *not* an expert—in the sense of being a particularly skilled researcher, a medical professional or even someone trained to speak with theological, thanatoric or any other authority.

But I am a storyteller and I believe in stories. I have spent a lifetime listening, interviewing, befriending and putting people at ease, in order to pass along their stories. There are those who leave this world better through the art they have created, the environment they have preserved or the discoveries they have made. There are others who leave only their stories. I believe the world is better for the stories that are left us.

Throughout the stories in this collection are suggestions for how we might model our own dying, how we might participate in the end-times of our own stories. Admittedly, chances for such participation are wildly varying. We might be wiped out by a drunk driver tonight or develop Alzheimer's or suffer a stroke tomorrow or find ourselves diagnosed with any of the still-incurable diseases next week. All of our stories, though, will have endings, *our very own* endings. And some stories have been left to us, by others, that address the ending process in ways we might want to know.

A couple I will call Dr. and Mrs. Greene were absolutely clear about the ending process of their lives, as clear and deliberate as they had been throughout long years of service to their fields and community and an extraordinary dedication to each other that spanned more than a half century. For a variety of reasons the family did not want their real name used. Their daughter, though, willingly shared the story and her own feelings of gratitude for the legacy her parents left in both living and dying.

The Greenes had each left their native Germany in the 1930s as the Nazi persecution of Jews escalated. A summa cum laude graduate of law school then working as a bank lawyer, Dr. Greene helped many other Jews liquidate assets and transfer property before he himself was forced to flee. Mrs. Greene came to the U.S. as a 16-year-old with her parents. The couple married shortly after she finished college, when he had already picked up another law degree in this country.

Throughout the fifty-four years of their marriage, the Greenes built impressive reputations in their careers—she as an art curator and he as a teacher and scholar in international and comparative law. But what was most impressive to many of their friends was their mutual devotion; after all those years "they were still like teenagers in love," said one.

Dr. Greene, by eleven years the elder of the two, had become legally blind shortly before his wife developed symptoms of an encroaching illness. They were both otherwise in good health, and "Mom was in great shape (at seventy-six)," their daughter recalls, "still striding around and active."

In July 1996, their daughter was with them when the doctors gave them the results of tests done on Mrs. Greene. The diagnosis was that she had the most lethal form of leukemia. As they left the office, the daughter says, "I thought I heard him lean down to say, 'I'm going with you'."

Mrs. Greene chose not to attempt any interventions, though her white blood cell count was zero. "Mom lived it out," her daughter says. "As long as there was one tiny iota of quality of life she was going for it. They had a mad scramble to bring their affairs to a close, but (Dad) had zero, no, not *any* interest in going on without her. They were perfectly clear that they would take their leave together."

A little more than three months after her diagnosis, during which time he had helped care for his wife, Dr. and Mrs. Greene were found lying side by side on their bed, glasses with a residue of white powder on each night table. They were holding hands.

The Greenes left what their daughter terms "very extraordinary communications" for their children and grandchildren, clear expressions of their devotion to each other and love for their family. Because of family and religious considerations, they chose not to talk openly about their decision. "But (my husband) and I felt blessed to have ushered them through those last months, and for every memory that we have."

I feel exactly the same about the death of my own father, the man who anchored my life for fifty-four years, up until the very moment he knelt to pray himself into the hereafter. Though he didn't need the further help of a lethal potion, his dying seemed both consistent with his life and as filled with meaning as the dying of the Greenes. It was as if he were saying, "OK, I've showed you everything I can about how to live; here is how to die."

Certainly it is never that simple. Few of us get to ordain the time and manner of our dying exactly as we would choose. But some of us seem to invest that time with great significance, to claim it as part of life itself. This kind of confrontation of one's own mortality is, unlike the despair that must accompany suicide, more akin to the dawn than to the sunset. Not a closing of life's final door as much as an opening.

This is true of a retiree named Michael Erlanger, whom I first met through several slim volumes of his poetry which were sent by a friend. Later he and I exchanged letters and phone calls in which he elaborated on his theories of living and dying.

Michael Erlanger first confronted his own mortality when he was in flight training with the U.S. Air Force in the 1940s. "I started out being terrified," he wrote later, "until I accepted the fact that I'd either be killed or I wouldn't. I never thought about it again."

Erlanger was not killed in his Air Force days. After the war, he went on to a successful career in the textile business. He raised a family, published several books of fiction and retired eventually to Athens, Georgia, where his wife was pursuing a graduate degree. Then, nearly fifty years after that early resolution of the terror that death presented, Erlanger faced it again. He credits Athens cardiologist Robert Sinyard and other medical professionals with "giving me years I didn't know I had" and he decided to use those years, in part, to express himself through poetry.

Songs of Aging came first, a small volume celebrating the joys and woes of simply surviving past one's life expectancy. "The logical step after *Songs of Aging*," Erlanger wrote in the introduction to his second book, "is Songs of Death, to be followed by Songs of Living, which can be about anything from rebirth after death to counting clouds. The alternative is Songs of Nothing. Here is *Continuum* which is my name for Songs of Death followed by Songs of Living. I have no idea how to write Songs of Nothing."

In *Continuum* Erlanger wrote:

> I started out to understand my date with death
> I found I didn't need one—we are to meet—
> but what I found was a rage against growing old
> and this I thought was wrapped and tied and put
>   away
> to find it only in my brain not in my guts
> It's out of storage now and ripe for understanding

Earlier, in *Songs of Aging* he had written:

You want to keep from growing old?
Die young.
You want to forget you're growing old?
Create

a song
a story
an idea
a new way of dressing
anything
absorb a cloud
absorb a tree
if you are where you can watch water
watch water
your life is changing
go with the change
milk it

Erlanger's poems are, he says, only a way of expressing himself. I think they also serve as a model, of sorts, for confronting one's end-of-life issues. In a different sense, the Greenes also created a model.

There are eloquent models created also by some whose dying came much too soon. My friend Ed Currie, mentioned in an earlier chapter, met his dying head on, exactly as he had lived.

Ed was part of a group of AIDS patients and their friends who met regularly to talk about how things were going, to enjoy dinner together and offer mutual support.

Tom, who would die a matter of weeks after Ed, was also a member of the group. Both had had successful careers and supportive family and friends.

Tom was possessed of a sharp wit and quick tongue, though he seldom used those gifts to brighten his own world. At a meeting only a few months before he and Ed would both die he spoke of his anger over an admittedly unkind fate and told at some length about how difficult he found the days to be.

Sitting next to Tom, Ed listened thoughtfully and commented as helpfully as possible. And then he said: "You know, this has been one of the best weeks of my life. I managed to get out to the movies Thursday, and haven't been in extraordinary pain. Day before yesterday I had this great idea. I got down all the boxes of old pictures—you know, the ones you stuff in shoeboxes and mean to do something with—and spent two entire days writing names and dates on the back, and notes about who the people were or what was going on. I really mean it, this has been one of the best weeks of my life."

Despite all attempts by his friends to break through, Tom was consumed by the anger and depression that walled him off until the day he died, alone. On the other hand Ed, I think, kept on making his weeks the best he could, moving steadily toward his dying by living as fully as possible.

Often, when moving toward their dying or discussing the prospect, people list being alone as the thing they fear the most. So it is not surprising to find how much comfort exists in having someone nearby—someone who can alleviate the pain, whether that pain is physical, spiritual or emotional.

When Lucy Cook died, not long ago in Decatur, Georgia, she had people who filled all of the above roles, and more.

Lucy's dying was a community experience, a time in which she and the unlikely group that gathered to surround her drew strength and peace from each other.

Mother of a young daughter, Lucy taught preaching and worship at Columbia Theological Seminary. She and her husband Gerry had for some years been part of a worshiping community centered around homelessness, an intimate group that was one of other, larger circles within their urban Presbyterian church. Their immediate household included two street people who had come into the family through the shelter program nine years earlier—"so there have always been a lot of hands," Gerry says, "a lot of people to help."

When a bone scan revealed cancer spread throughout her body, Lucy was devastated. But she knew what to do with that sadness: she shared it with what Gerry defines as "the community." And for a year, they then became part of the process.

As her health deteriorated Lucy fought back, not for the cure she knew to be beyond reach but for a strengthened quality of life. With the seminary's help she gave up everything but the small-group work she loved most. A classroom aide was brought in to make things as easy as possible. "Paradoxically," Gerry says, "the disease released her from stress and enabled her to experience herself more fully." The two of them also grew closer and more trusting of shared emotions.

In the spring of her last year, Lucy's community of friends grew closer too, taking turns with whatever needed to be done or simply being together. Gerry left his own teaching job so he could be with her and their eight-year-old daughter.

By June of 1996 Lucy had begun a precipitous decline, and the word went out to those who were not in the immediate community circle. Her parents and siblings came, and friends who had not seen her for a while joined those who had remained nearby. "Every night people would come," Gerry says, "and there would be singing. Lucy was so full of grace and peace.

"I think this is symbolic of the way things were: on the night before she died I'd gone into the other room to get some sleep. About 1 a.m. I woke up and went into the room where Lucy was. There were four people sitting around in chairs, singing to each other.

"She died about 6 a.m., but we didn't call the funeral home until that evening. All day, and into the evening, people came, until there were about fifty-five people here. When they carried her out, about nine that night, everybody had lined up between the porch and the house, and we sang 'I'll Fly Away.' She had been lucid until just the last few hours, talking to people, knowing that everyone was with her."

Gerry Cook believes that the powerful elements of his wife's dying were the sense of community that continually surrounded her, "all of us needing all of us," and the intimate sharing of emotions. "There were people with many different understandings of faith, including a Hindu priest," he says; "Lucy's gift was accepting people as they were."

When his wife's long struggle was over, Cook says, their daughter began her own struggle with what it would be like without her mom. "But there was never a sense, for her, that the things going on were not normal, that there was anything to fear."

The message Lucy Cook and the rest of her family and friends gave to her daughter is the message left by those in virtually all of the stories here: dying may not be something we want, but it need not be something we fear. Michael E. Brown, a young man in San Francisco who was diagnosed as HIV-positive in the mid-1980s (and is alive and well at the time of this writing,) took an activist approach to facing a possible early death. In 1995, he sent out a fund-raising letter before setting out on a 525-mile bicycle ride from San Francisco to Los Angeles to raise money for the non-profit San Francisco AIDS Foundation. The letter, he said later, was simply an attempt to explain his own feelings about living with the constant threat of death.

"AIDS has taught me many things," Michael wrote, "including strength, perseverance, compassion, hope, patience and love. It has also taught me to be fearless. A teacher by the name of Baba Muktananda said, 'There are only two things that inspire fear. The first is that you are not aware of the divine place of fearlessness inside you. The other is that you are not aware of God's help.'

"I believe there's a divine place of fearlessness inside all of us. With help from each other, I believe we find that place."

People much older than Michael, when expressing their thoughts about death and dying, often list "fear of nursing home" simultaneously with "fear of being alone." Today, healthy at sixty-five, I think "fear of nursing home" is closest to the top of my list. But one man who died recently in a California nursing home did so remarkably without loneliness and, I think, also without fear. His story was told by *San Francisco Chronicle* columnist Joan Ryan, his daughter-in-law.

"My mother-in-law is holding my father-in-law's limp hand, which is puffy from fluids pooling under the skin," Ryan wrote of those final days in the nursing home. "She pats the hand, then strokes his face with the backs of her fingers. He's in a restless sleep. Sometimes his eyebrows furrow. Sometimes his good hand flies up to his eye and rubs hard. Or he tries to pull the oxygen tubes out of his nose.

"'Oh, no you don't, darling,' my mother-in-law says, pulling his hand away and laying it back on the sheets.

"She arrives every day at 11 and leaves every day at 4. 'Oh, sweetheart,' she sighs, standing by the bed, studying the man she married more than sixty years ago. He was old school. He never wanted her to learn to drive or pay the bills. When they grew older, he would line up her pills on the breakfast table every day to make sure she didn't forget any. He never forgot to open the car door for her. He told her he loved her every night before they went to sleep and every morning when they awoke. Even in their eighties, they still held hands."

The family, Ryan wrote, decided against inserting a feeding tube when the doctors said it would prolong the inevitable. "They would keep him comfortable with an IV of nutrients, and morphine when necessary." Still, her mother-in-law anguished, wondering if she were doing everything right, if he could get better after all.

"Sometimes I'd look at my father-in-law and suddenly see myself," Ryan wrote, "an old woman incapacitated by a dreadful disease. I'd look at my mother-in-law and hope someone would still be around to hover over me, to pat my arm and swab my dry lips, to make sure the morphine dosage was sufficient and the nurses washed my hair even if I didn't notice.

"Though my father-in-law sank deeper into his coma and his breath grew labored, I knew he was one of the luckiest men in the building. His happy life didn't shrink to the size of a wheelchair, a man imprisoned in a useless body. He suffered the stroke on a golf course, doing what he enjoyed. And five weeks later, a month shy of his eighty-ninth birthday, he slipped away in his sleep, doted on and babied and loved.

"Part of our fear of dying, I think, is that we have to do it alone. But I know now that isn't true. My father-in-law died as he had lived, hand-in-hand with his very best friend."

The same was true for my friend Margaret Spaulding's aunt and uncle, whose living and dying continue to impact Margaret's life.

Much more than an aunt, Mildred Brune was a mentor, friend and philosophical correspondent when Margaret was a young mother in Berkeley, California, raising her only daughter in the early 1970s. Aunt Mildred was herself living in southern Florida at the time, with her beloved husband Walter. Her letters crossing the country are filled with reflections, remembrances of her own youth in the San Francisco Bay Area, and contemplation of the meaning of life and death. References to books that Mildred and Margaret were reading also flew back and forth. It was as if the two women, of two different generations, were on parallel journeys of discovery.

In February 1973, Aunt Mildred wrote of "an exercise in dis-identification" that she and Uncle Walter were reading about in *Psychosynthesis* by Roberto Assagioli M.D.: "I am not my body—that's obvious enough—I *have* emotions but I am not my emotions . . . I *have* an intellect, but am not my intellect . . . I am just 'a center of pure consciousness.' And now all I've got to do is find out what under the sun is that!" She reflects further on how the words of Taoism help her in believing "a strong desire for a good thing will work itself out if you, yourself, just help in a sort of rhythm with natural forces."

In another letter the same month, Aunt Mildred refers to the parallel journeys: "It's been like a window you scrubbed bright and clear and we love what we see through it—a young woman (you) searching, sifting values and not sure of anything. Please never, never be sure of anything." But for herself, she says, "I must simplify things to this: do the best I can with the present moment . . . "

Simplifying, for Mildred and Walter, soon became a matter of divesting themselves of "things," major properties and small, meaningful items alike. Aunt Mildred explains in her letters that "things" have become a burden, somewhat akin to a quotation she likes about love, "Belief clings, faith lets go." Increasingly, she and Walter want to let go of a world in which they no longer believe. They are distressed by the Watergate-era political news, by increasing crime, overpopulation and pollution, and by their helplessness to reverse those tides.

Aunt Mildred eventually discloses, in the letters, that her beloved Walter is living with an arterial aneurysm which could rupture at any moment, resulting in a swift and painful death. When it was diagnosed, three years earlier, they chose not to have the risky surgery that might well have left him an invalid and decided instead to enjoy what time they had together.

"We thought at first that we could 'forget'," she writes, "and go about as usual, but we learned very soon that we couldn't. Going for a quiet little lunch in a nice restaurant was shadowed by fear neither of us could 'forget.' And so we withdrew completely from the outside world. I too, for I have not a moment's peace when I am away from him.

"Lest you think by now that we have had three fearladen and dreary years," she continues, "I want to make the picture a true one for you . . . we have found more joy in being together than in our heretofore happy years of health. We are nearer and dearer to each other with every day of being together and in our books, our own experiences, we have developed a Faith (capital F) that not only is sustaining but makes our world a wonderful thing." There remains only the burden of their "things."

"And now, what to do?," Aunt Mildred muses in writing, as Walter's time continues to run out and her own health weakens to the point at which her energy only takes her through the first few hours of the morning. "On Wednesday of this week we arranged with a moving company to ship our things to you later this year—probably in late October (we can't set a definite time, for the date must depend upon when we can make definite plans for our own future.) We have a great change in our living scheme of things and must go step by step and live with happy memories of family and friends and happy times in the past—as we do, with great gratitude in our hearts."

The news of the moving company did not quite come out of the blue. In earlier letters Aunt Mildred had sounded Margaret out for her willingness to provide a new home for their treasures. She also provided background materials. In one letter came a photo of a bowl decorated with shells and a porcelain lobster, set atop their TV. It dated back to the days when Mildred and Walter used to enjoy playing the horses at small tracks in Maryland and Virginia. "One day (Walter) won a whale of a bet," she wrote in the accompanying letter, "and spent it on a lobster bowl I had a whale of a wish for."

On October 9, Aunt Mildred sent a letter telling Margaret the packers and movers had come and gone, and "an unusually nice and friendly man, Archie" would be delivering them, after an advance 24-hour notice, to California. A letter dated October 12 follows, with the information that Mildred and Walter "have reservations for Monday at Schraffts Motor Inn, East Sunrise and Atlantic Avenue," and giving the name and address of their attorney. It concludes, "Think of us always—with arms about our two girls."

Days later, at about the time their worldly goods arrived on the West Coast, Mildred and Walter were found dead, of natural causes, at their Florida home. A letter Margaret had sent to the Motor Inn was later returned. Margaret never knew whether those reservations were part of a plan, later changed, to end their lives in that place, or part of an intention simply to get away from home as their "things" were leaving. What she does know is that their poignant message of care and affection for "our two girls" was the last communication sent across the country from her Aunt Mildred.

Did Mildred and Walter Brune or Ed Currie or Earl Moreland or any of the others whose stories appear within these pages, knowingly live their lives into the exact moment of their dying? We cannot know. What we can know is that they met their dying head-on, with the resources available to them, and though they had no yearning for that moment to come they showed no fear of its approach. Somehow, in all of these stories the absence of fear of dying seems to go hand in hand with the presence of joy of living.

Michael Erlanger summed it up this way in *Songs of Aging*, with a poem that could apply for any age:

> The years of life pay off
> I can now sing a song of forgiveness
> and it follows I can sing an I-Like-Me song
> I am a self-contained musical comedy
> ready and able to sing away
>
> And when I sing my song of death
> I'll shout it from my very core
> and when the coda's sung
> I'll stop singing
> till then let my songs of aging soar
> Hallelujah.

Acknowledgements

I am immeasurably indebted to the people whose stories make up this book, courageous participants in their own final days. Friends and loved ones of many of them graciously shared stories and insights with me and without their generous and thoughtful contributions the book would not have been possible. Although the stories are briefly told, in many cases those contributions involved lengthy and/or repeated interviews. In every case I was met with kindness and courtesy. To those whose names appear throughout the book I am particularly grateful.

Six years in creation, *Dying Unafraid* would never have made it past the first tentative days without the support of friends, many of them writers, who offered encouragement and suggestions, put me in contact with potential stories and generally saw the project and its author as better than we deserved. Among the writers I am particularly grateful to Annie Lamott, who first insisted I could be a Real Writer if I chose, and to my irreplaceable friends and fellow literary travelers Liz Randal, Claudia Madison, Gail Manning, Diane Rosenbloom, Tessa Melvin, Caiti Collins, Martha Klopfer, Frances Burch and Anna Villegas. Ted Williams was amazingly kind and helpful to a writer he'd never met or heard of before. The repeated assurance from friends and strangers alike that the concept of *Dying Unafraid* was valid and potentially useful, and the long-distance enthusiasm of my children, Skip Fossett, Sandy O'Brien and Pam Wilson, has been a source of inspiration and joy.

Many whose work demands care and understanding of the dying shared insights, and often stories, with me. Board members, staff and volunteers with Compassion in Dying; Director Maureen Redl of Voices of Healing (as well as a number of VOH participants); and Executive Director Charlotte Ross of Death with Dignity National Center all offered the benefits of their experience and wisdom. Kaiser Permanente Hospice Program Director Richard Brett, Director Joanne Lynn of The Center to Improve Care of the Dying, *Sequoia* Editor Robert Forsberg, Paradigm founder and Director Richard Wagner and Executive Director William Glenn of Continuum generously took time to answer questions and give suggestions. I received help and encouragement also from the Rev. Dr. Laird Stuart, Lee and Wes Hinton, Patrick Thornton, Nancy Jaicks, Dr. Marilyn Washburn, Dr. Lee Stone and Dr. Michaela Glenn. Stories and helpful commentary came from Jim Crawford, Carol Rush, Mark

Leno, Ralph Mero, Pauline Birtwistle and the late Jan de Blieck. Members of the HIV Support Group of Calvary Presbyterian Church have been the best ongoing support group anyone ever had.

I want to thank Anne Ricks Sumers, Eugene Methvin and Joan Ryan for permission to use their stories which appeared earlier in *Newsweek*, *The Wall Street Journal* and *The San Francisco Chronicle*.

Friends and family who cheered me on, forwarded suggestions and even introduced me to the internet include Mimi Smith, Pat French, Miles O'Brien, Ann McDowell, Pat Funk, Rosalyn Cothran, Dr. Ben Branscomb and Rachel Henning. Jane Dystel's faith and encouragement were of inestimable value at a critical time.

These and many others have made working on *Dying Unafraid* a great joy. It would never have been possible, though, without the love, consideration and tireless support of The Great Encourager, Bud Johns.